Crafts

CRAFTS in a FLASH!

quick, quicker & quickest projects

COWLES
Creative Publishing, Inc.

Copyright© 1998 Cowles Creative Publishing, Inc.
5900 Green Oak Drive, Minnetonka, Minnesota 55343 • 1-800-328-3895 • All rights reserved • Printed in U.S.A.

Contents

Quickest

Quicker

Quick

Quickest!

Need a last-minute gift? Want a new look on the dining room table right now? Find ideas a-plenty on the following pages, such as candles, jewelry, wearables, tabletop and storage items and picture frames. All can be completed with

a minimum of time—an evening, afternoon or half an hour every day for a week if there's paint and glue to dry. Best of all, even though they don't take long to make, these items look so great you'll proudly say you made them yourself.

Modern MINI CLOCKS

The thought of being a clock maker is very daunting: however, it is extremely easy to put together clock components. That leaves just the fun and fast part of decorating. Here are three different styles: a modern gift-wrap decoupage finish; a faux marquetry finish, resembling inlaid wood; and a star-studded gold-foiled finish.

LIST of MATERIALS

For All Clocks
* 1 unpainted wooden mini clock, (6" x 3" or 4" x 1.25")*
* 1 mini clock movement (1.4375" diameter)*
* Craft knife, cutting surface
* Paintbrushes: ¾" (2 cm) sponge brush, small brush

For Decoupaged Clock
* Metallic copper acrylic paint
* Wrapping or tissue paper
* Decoupage medium

For Faux Marquetry Clock
* Stain markers in 4 or more different colors
* Water-base varnish

For Gold-Foiled Clock
* Navy blue wood stain or cold-water fabric dye
* Painter's masking tape
* Gold foil and foil adhesive
* Miscellaneous items: paint palette, fine sandpaper, tack cloth, ruler, pencil, craft glue

*(See Sources on pg. 159 for purchasing information.)

FOR ALL CLOCKS

Refer to page 156 for Painting Instructions and Techniques. Lightly sand all surfaces of clock; remove dust with tack cloth. Use sponge brush to basecoat Gold-Foiled Clock with navy blue following manufacturer's instructions and Decoupage Clock with metallic copper. To complete each clock, install the clock movement into the clock cavity.

DECOUPAGED CLOCK

1 *Lay clock flat* on its back on wrapping or tissue paper, and trace around the clock onto paper with a pencil. Carefully cut out the tracing with a craft knife or scissors. Apply decoupage medium with sponge brush to clock face following manufacturer's instructions; do not get medium into clock cavity. Place wrapping paper on medium. See illustration to gently smooth out any bubbles or wrinkles; apply more medium per manufacturer's recommendations.

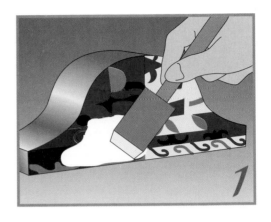

2 *Repeat Step 1* for clock back, if desired. Cut a strip 1/2" (1.3 cm) wide, and long enough to go along top and side edges. Repeat Step 1 to decoupage strip along top and side edges. Let dry; carefully cut paper around clock cavity.

FAUX MARQUETRY CLOCK

1 *Refer to photo and illustration* to use a ruler and lightly pencil in lines on top and side edges of clock, approximately 1" (2.5 cm) apart. Begin at clock top in center and go down each side. Mark a border line along top and sides of clock front 1/2" (1.3 cm) in from edge. Bring side edge lines down to this border line.

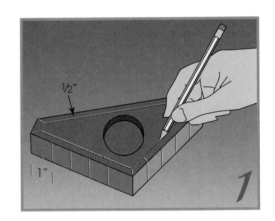

2 *Use ruler and craft knife* to lightly score the pencil lines, just deep enough to keep the stain from spreading.

3 *Use stain markers* to tint the scored-off areas. Follow marker manufacturer's instructions for usage and drying times. Add more coats as desired; let dry. Apply 1 or more coats of varnish with sponge brush; let dry.

GOLD-FOILED CLOCK

1 *Place 2 pieces* of tape along top and sides of clock so a 1/2" (1.3 cm) center stripe is created. Follow manufacturer's instructions to apply foil adhesive. When adhesive is dry, but still tacky, remove tape. Apply gold foil to stripe following manufacturer's instructions.

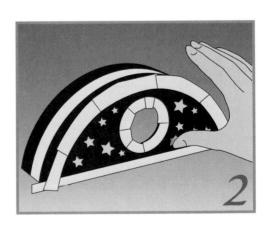

2 *Refer to photo and illustration* to use masking tape to create a 3/8" (1 cm) border along clock face and around clock movement cavity. Pinch the excess tape together on inside edges to ease tape along curves. Cut small stars from masking tape and apply randomly over clock face, or you can also use star stickers or stencils. Repeat Step 1 to apply foil adhesive, remove tape and stars, and apply gold foil.

Dried Bean DECORATIONS

Fill a bowl with round and egg-shaped Dried Bean Decorations for an interesting centerpiece, or display the bean-covered cone instead. Nothing could be simpler or less expensive than gluing various colored peas, beans and lentils to papier mâché forms.

* Papier mâché shapes: 3" x 13½" (7.5 x 34.3 cm) cone; 3" x 5" (7.5 x 12.5 cm) egg; 2" x 3" (5 x 7.5 cm) egg; two 2½" (6.5 cm) balls
* Dried beans and peas: green split peas, yellow split peas, lentils, small red chili beans, black beans, great northern beans, red kidney beans, pinto beans, navy beans, black-eyed peas, pink beans
* Extra-thick acrylic spray finish
* Thick white craft glue
* Miscellaneous items: craft stick, wax paper, ruler, pencil

1 Green Spit Peas
2 Yellow Split Peas
3 Lentils
4 Small Red Chili Beans
5 Black Beans
6 Great Northern Beans
7 Red Kidney Beans
8 Pinto Beans
9 Navy Beans
10 Black-Eyed Peas
11 Pink Beans

1 *Assembly:* Use craft stick to spread glue on each shape as you work on it. Glue beans according to instructions; let dry on wax paper for 24 hours. Spray with several coats of finish.

2 *Cone:* Refer to the photo and Assembly Guide to mark wide patterned bands on cone with pencil and ruler. Glue rows of beans, beginning at the bottom. When covering tlp, glue 1 green split pea at the top, then glue spiral bands downward to line 4.

3 *Large Egg:* Begin at the wide end with a green split pea encircled by black beans. Refer to the illustration to glue beans in rows as follows: 11, 10, 2, 5, 8, 1, 6, 2, 5, 3, 7, 10, 1, 5, 9. Glue 2 red kidney beans on the end.

4 *Striped Ball:* Begin at 1 end with a black bean encircled by navy beans. Refer to the illustration to glue beans in rows as follows: 4, 8, 5, 11, 4, 8, 5, 9. Glue 1 small red chili bean on the end.

5 *Small Egg and Green Ball:* Cover egg with navy beans and ball with green split peas.

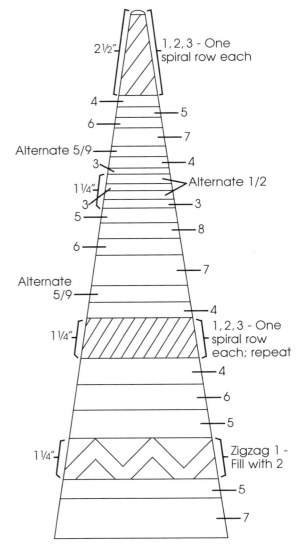

2½"
1, 2, 3 - One spiral row each
4
5
6
7
Alternate 5/9
4
3
Alternate 1/2
1¼"
3
3
5
8
6
7
Alternate 5/9
4
1¼"
1, 2, 3 - One spiral row each; repeat
4
6
5
1¼"
Zigzag 1 - Fill with 2
5
7

ASSEMBLY GUIDE

Star OF THE PARTY

Dress up for any special event in this glittery shirt you make yourself by simply stenciling stars on a tuxedo shirt.

LIST of MATERIALS

* White tuxedo shirt
* Stencil adhesive spray
* Star stencils
* Silver metallic paint creme
* Multicolor confetti brush-on fabric paint
* Paintbrushes: small stencil, 1" (2.5 cm) sponge brush
* Miscellaneous items: T-shirt board, masking tape, paper towels

1 *Follow manufacturer's instructions* to wash and press shirt; do not use fabric softener. Mount shirt on T-shirt board.

2 *Spray stencil adhesive* on back of stencil and let dry until tacky. Starting at right shoulder, position stencil diagonally on shirt. Prepare paint creme according to manufacturer's instructions.

3 *To stencil,* pick up very little paint on brush and move on paper towel in a circular motion to evenly distribute paint. With brush straight up and down and bristles flat on fabric, apply paint with a circular motion. Stencil stars leaving center of large stars unpainted. Reposition stencil several times to create a flow of stars from right shoulder to lower left side of shirt. Also stencil a small star on each collar point. Let dry 24 hours.

4 *To decorate shirt,* scoop confetti paint onto sponge brush and spread onto shirt over stenciled stars including collar points. Let dry 6 hours, then repeat. Launder shirt according to fabric paint manufacturer's instructions.

Doilies
SWEATSHIRT

This sweatshirt is the best choice for casual wear—decorated with coordinating fabric napkins and a dish towel and embellished with lacy doilies.

LIST of MATERIALS

❊ Sweatshirt
❊ Coordinating plaid woven napkins, two
❊ Coordinating plaid woven dish towel
❊ White crochet doilies: 6" (15 cm) square; 4" (10 cm) heart; 1½" to 2½" (3.8 to 6.5 cm) round, three (See Sources on pg. 159 for purchasing information.)
❊ Fusible web
❊ Sewing threads: white, matching colors
❊ Washable fabric glue (optional)
❊ Miscellaneous items: iron, ruler, pencil, scissors, straight pins, zigzag sewing machine, sewing needle (optional)

1 *Follow manufacturer's instructions* to apply fusible web to wrong side of napkins and towel. Cut a 6" (15 cm) square from fused towel, a 3" x 6" (7.5 x 15 cm) rectangle from fused napkin and a 6½" x 6½" x 9½" (16.3 x 16.3 x 24.3 cm) corner triangle from remaining fused napkin.

2 *Refer to the photo* to position and fuse fabrics on sweatshirt.

3 *Cut 6" (15 cm) square doily* to fit inside corner triangle; pin. Use matching threads to machine-appliqué the cut edges of fused fabrics; see illustration. Straight-stitch finished sides of triangle.

4 *Refer to the photo* to glue or stitch lace doilies in place on towel square and rectangle napkin.

SACHETS

*F*lower thread and delicate cross-stitches fashion lovely linen sachets.

LIST of MATERIALS

For Each Sachet
❋ 28-count beige linen, 5¼" x 7¼" (13.2 x 18.7 cm)
❋ 1 skein each of DMC flower thread in colors listed on Color Key
❋ No. 24 tapestry needle
❋ ⅛" (3 mm) pink satin ribbon, ½ yd. (0.5 m)
❋ Potpourri
❋ Pattern Sheet
❋ Miscellaneous items: scissors, matching sewing thead and needle, two terrycloth towels, iron

1 *Preparation:* Refer to page 155 for Cross-Stitch Instructions and Stitches and pattern sheet for charts. Each square on the charts represents 2 threads of linen and symbols correspond to flower thread colors.

2 *Work cross-stitches* with 1 strand of flower thread over 2 threads of linen, making sure to work initial stitch over a vertical thread. Work Smyrna crosses over 6 threads of linen. Do not carry thread over more than 4 threads of linen. Fold linen in half and lightly crease. On left half, measure 1¾" (4.5 cm) from top and 1" (2.5 cm) from side and begin stitching at this point. (If necessary, move over 1 thread to begin stitching over a vertical thread.)

3 *Finishing:* Use a warm iron to press the stitched design facedown between towels. Pull threads at the top edge to fringe ¾" (2 cm).

4 *Assembly:* Fold linen in half, right sides together, and stitch ¼" (6 mm) side and bottom seams with tiny running stitches. Turn right side out. Thread tapestry needle with ribbon and, starting at side seam, carefully weave ribbon around top, ½" (1.3 cm) below fringe. Fill sachet with potpourri and tie ribbon ends in a bow.

Nature's SCENTS

The Woodland Crossing

recipe blends pine, mint and allspice into a hearty, masculine scent, while Lavender Passion combines rose petals, lavender and other herbs and spices for a subtle feminine fragrance. Display potpourri in sachet bags, crystal bowls, decorative boxes, antique teacups and even seashells.

1 *Dry Ingredients:* Combine dry ingredients, except orris root, 1 at a time, and gently mix with wood spoon after each 1 is added. Add orris root, which acts as a fixative, and gently mix.

2 *Oils:* Add oil(s), 1 drop at a time, mixing gently after each drop. For Lavender Passion, add 15 drops of lavender oil. For Woodland Crossing, add 10 pine oil drops and 5 patchouli oil drops.

3 *Setting the Scents:* Fill glass jars with potpourri and tightly screw on lids. Store jars in a cool, dark place for 3-6 weeks, opening occasionally to stir contents. Fill sachet bags or selected containers with potpourri, and enjoy.

LIST of MATERIALS

For Either Potpourri
* 1/8 cup (25 mL) orris root (use ground orris root for sachet potpourri and chopped root for potpourri displayed in a glass or open container)
* Sachet or container of your choice

For Lavender Passion Potpourri, Approximately 4 Cups (1 L)
* Dried flowers, leaves and moss: 2 cups (500 mL) lavender buds and leaves; 1/2 cup (125 mL) statice; 1/4 cup (50 mL) cornflowers; 1/4 cup (50 mL) crushed rose petals; 1/4 cup (50 mL) rose-scented geranium leaves; 1/2 cup (125 mL) oakmoss
* Spices: 1 tablespoon (15 mL) each whole allspice and whole cloves; 1 teaspoon (5 mL) ground cinnamon
* Lavender-scented oil

For Woodland Crossing Potpourri, Approximately 6 Cups (1.5 L)
* Dried flowers, leaves and pinecones: 1/3 cup (75 mL) calendula petals; 1 cup (250 mL) each crushed peppermint leaves and crushed spearmint leaves; 2 cups (500 mL) crushed pine needles; 1 1/2 cups (375 mL) hemlock pinecones
* Spices: 1 tablespoon (15 mL) whole allspice; 1/4 cup (50 mL) rosemary leaves
* Scented oils: pine, patchouli
* Miscellaneous items: large ceramic or stainless steel mixing bowl, measuring cups and spoons, wood mixing spoon, large glass jars with tight lids

Colorful CANDLEHOLDERS

For easy but beautiful candleholders, glue tissue paper to the outside of glass containers. Use glowing, warm paper for a look reminiscent of stained glass, or a delicate, pale design for a quiet romantic mood. Other ideas for containers are fishbowls, vases or mason jars.

LIST of MATERIALS

* ❋ Glass container, suitable for candles
* ❋ Tissue paper or translucent decorative paper: green, purple, pink, blue
* ❋ Thick white craft glue or decoupage medium
* ❋ Acrylic sealer
* ❋ Pillar candle
* ❋ 1" (2.5 cm) sponge brush
* ❋ Small rhinestones or decorative gems (optional)
* ❋ Miscellaneous items: scissors, wax paper, bowl or container

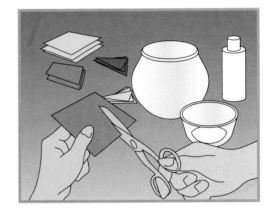

1 *Preparation:* Wash and dry candleholder thoroughly. Remove any labels and label residue. Cut or tear the tissue paper into small pieces approximately 1" to 1½" (2.5 to 3.8 cm), varying shapes and sizes as desired. Lay out in piles near the candleholder, as shown in the illustration.

2 *Gluing:* Thin the craft glue with water until it is of a milky consistency. Place a piece of wax paper flat to use as a gluing surface. Lay a cut piece of tissue paper facedown on wax paper, and apply a thin layer of glue, using sponge brush. See the Step 2 illustration.

3 *Application:* Position the paper on the outside of the candleholder. Gently smooth it in place using your finger. Be careful not to move it too much, or the paper might tear. Continue applying pieces of tissue randomly, overlapping as desired, until the container is covered.

4 *Finishing:* See the illustration to wrap paper around the upper edge of the container as well, to cover the rim on the inside. Apply a light coat of acrylic sealer. Let dry and apply a second coat. If desired, glue on rhinestones or other gems. Let dry, and place candle in candleholder.

*S*unflower
JAR TOPPER

***S*imply zigzag stitching** elastic on the inside of the sunflower petals and center makes this jar topper, which can dress up a pint of homemade jelly, canned tomatoes or even a button collection.

LIST of MATERIALS

* Regular-mouth canning jar with lid
* Cotton mini print fabrics: 5" (12.5 cm) square brown check; 9" x 18" (23 x 46 cm) gold
* 1/4" (6 mm) elastic, 1/4 yd. (0.25 m)
* Pattern Sheet
* Miscellaneous items: tracing paper, pencil, scissors, sewing needle, matching thread, zigzag sewing machine, straight pins

1 *Trace the petal pattern* and cut out from gold fabric. Cut a 4 1/2" (11.5 cm) circle from brown check. Stack petal pieces on top of each other, alternating petals.

2 *Position center circle* over petals and baste close to outside edge. Using basting line as placement guide, zigzag elastic to wrong side of flower, stretching elastic while sewing. Stretch finished topper over jar lid.

Sunshine SUNFLOWER PLACE CARDS

*B*righten up the table

with these easy-to-make place cards and after the meal, give each guest a personalized mini plant to take home as a memento of the event.

LIST *of* MATERIALS

For Each Place Card

❈ Gold mini print fabric, 3" (7.5 cm) squares, two
❈ Fusible web, 3" (7.5 cm) square
❈ ⅞" (2.2 cm) brown button
❈ 2" (5 cm) clay flowerpot
❈ Fine-point permanent black marker
❈ Floral foam, 1½" (3.8 cm) square
❈ 4" (10 cm) cinnamon stick
❈ Spanish moss
❈ Natural raffia, 8" (20.5 cm) strand
❈ Hot glue gun
❈ Miscellaneous items: pencil, scissors, craft knife, ruler, tracing paper

FLOWER PATTERN

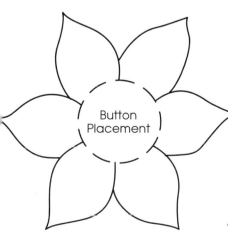

Button Placement

1 *Follow manufacturer's instructions* to fuse fabric squares together, right side out, with fusible web. Trace the pattern and cut from fabric. Glue button to center of flower and shape the sunflower petals by bending them forward around the button.

2 *Push and glue* the foam into the flowerpot. Use the black marker to print guest's name on the flowerpot rim.

3 *Glue 1 end* of the cinnamon stick to sunflower back and the opposite end centered in the foam. Cover the foam with Spanish moss. Tie raffia bow around cinnamon stick.

Stamped Apple
KITCHEN ACCESSORIES

Apples are longtime favorites for decorating, because of their bright, cheery color, their wonderful easy-to-make-shape and the memories they bring—like autumn, apple pie and bonfires. These stamped floor cloth, placemats and coasters are no exception; and inexpensive to boot, because you use an apple and a potato as the stampers.

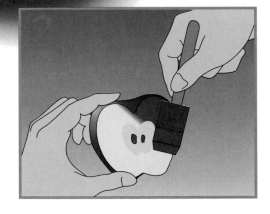

LIST of MATERIALS

* Kreative Kanvas™ half-moon floor cloth, placemats and coasters*
* 1 apple
* 1 potato
* Acrylic craft paints: Christmas green, alizarin crimson
* Gesso: white, unbleached titanium*
* Waterbase varnish
* 1" (2.5 cm) sponge brush
* Miscellaneous items: tracing paper, pencil, paring knife, paint palette

*(See Sources on pg. 159 for purchasing information.)

LEAF PATTERN

1 Preparation: Refer to pg. 156 for Painting Instructions and Techniques. Mix equal amounts of white and unbleached titanium gesso. Follow manufacturer's instructions to basecoat placemats, coasters and floor cloth with this mixture. Let dry, and apply a second coat. Let dry.

2 *Apple Stamp:* Cut apple in half vertically. Mix 2 parts crimson paint with 1 part varnish on paint palette. See Step 2 illustration to use sponge brush to apply mixture evenly to cut area of apple. Stamp apple on floor cloth. Reapply paint as needed, and continue stamping apples on floor cloth randomly. Refer to photo for placement. Stamp apples on placemats and coasters.

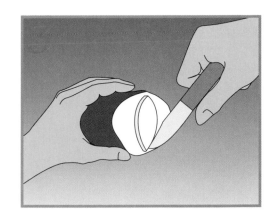

3 *Leaf Stamp:* Trace leaf pattern to tracing paper. Cut potato in half; transfer leaf design to cut side of potato. Use paring knife to cut away potato, leaving leaf design, as shown in illustration. Cut a straight line from 1 leaf tip to the other for vein line.

4 *Stamping Leaf:* Mix 2 parts green paint with 1 part varnish on paint palette. Stamp leaves on floor cloth, placemats and coasters; refer to photo and Step 4 illustration. Let dry.

5 *Finishing:* When paint is completely dry follow manufacturer's instructions to apply a coat of varnish to the front of all accessories. Continue to apply varnish until you have 4-5 coats, following manufacturer's recommended drying time between coats.

*C*rochet
LAMP SHADE COVER-UP

*A*n all-over mesh crochet pattern creates a lacy
elegant design to cover an entire lamp shade. Single crochet
and picots are perfect for a beginner and a snap for a pro.
Top it off with a row of premade lace for a decorator look.

LIST of MATERIALS

* 14" (35.5 cm) white linen lamp shade
* 2 skeins 200-yd. (184 m) size 10 ecru mercerized cotton crochet thread
* No. 6 steel crochet hook
* 2 yd. (1.85 m) ½" (1.3 cm) ecru lace
* White craft glue
* Miscellaneous items: scissors, ruler, spring clothespins

1 *General:* Refer to page 154 for Crochet Abbreviations and Stitches.

Gauge: 7 sc equals 1" (2.5 cm)

Finished Size: 8½" x 16" x 11½" (21.8 x 40.5 x 29.3 cm)

2 *Crocheting Lampshade:*

Ch 201
Rnd 1: 1 sc in 2nd ch from hook. * 1 sc in next ch, rep from * to end. To make a ring, sc in 1st sc: do not let it twist.

Rnd 2: * Ch 5, sk 3 sc, (1 sc, ch 3, 1 sc) in next sc. Rep from * around. End with (1 sc, ch 3, 1 sc) in last sc.

Rnd 3: Sl st into next st 3 times, ch 3, 1 sc in same ch, * ch 5, (1 sc, ch 3, 1 sc) in 3rd ch of next ch-5, rep from * around.

Rnd 4: * Ch-5, (1 sc, ch 3, 1 sc) in 3rd ch of next ch-5, rep from * around.

Rnds 5-26: Rep Rnd 4.

Rnd 27: * Ch 7, (1 sc, ch 3, 1 sc) in 3rd ch of next ch-5, rep from * around.

Rnd 28: * Ch 7, (1 sc, ch 3, 1 sc) in 4th ch of next ch-7, rep from * around.

Rnds 29-47: Rep Rnd 28. Fasten off.

3 *Finishing:* Slip the crocheted cover over the lamp shade and glue top edge of cover to the shade; let dry. Glue bottom edge to shade. Secure with clothespins; let dry. Remove clothespins. Glue lace around top and bottom edge of lamp shade and let dry.

Beaded Bracelet
WATCH

*N*owadays, many people have a collection of watches to coordinate with their wardrobe. In no "time," you can transform an inexpensive watch into a designer accessory by fashioning a band from beautiful beads.

LIST of MATERIALS

* 1¼" (3.2 cm) gold woman's watch
* ½" (1.3 cm) frosted crystal nugget beads, four*
* 18 x 8 mm rectangle beads, two each: teal and oriental jade*
* 14 x 10 mm frosted grape oval beads, three*
* 8 mm frosted grape cube beads, two*
* 7 mm round beads: two gold-washed, and four each frosted grape, teal and oriental jade*
* 4 mm gold-washed round beads, four*

* Gold-washed drum beads: 13 x 8 mm floral, two; 8 x 6 mm, six*
* 8 mm gold-washed ring beads, eight*
* 7 mm gold-washed floral spacer beads, 22*
* Gold elastic beading cord, 1½ yd. (1.4 m)
* White craft glue
* Miscellaneous items: scissors, ruler

*(See Sources on pg. 159 for purchasing information.)

1 *Remove spring bars* on watch where band attaches and thread two 4 mm round beads on each; replace bars.

2 *Cut an 18" (46 cm) cord piece* and tie a slipknot 3" (7.5 cm) from one end. See the Assembly Guide to string the first 4 beads in Row 1. Wrap cord end around spring bar outside gold beads and thread back through beads.

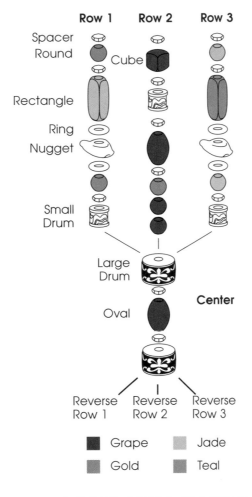

| Row 1 | Row 2 | Row 3 |

Spacer
Round   Cube
Rectangle
Ring
Nugget
Small
Drum
Large
Drum   Center
Oval
Reverse   Reverse   Reverse
Row 1   Row 2   Row 3

- Grape   Jade
- Gold   Teal

ASSEMBLY GUIDE

3 *Continue stringing Row 1 beads,* then center beads. Complete the row by adding Row 1 beads in reverse order. Wrap cord around opposite spring bar and back through beads. Untie slipknot, pulling cord ends to remove slack. Check fit on wrist, adding or subtracting beads as necessary. Knot cord and spot-glue. Trim cord, concealing ends inside beads.

4 *Repeat Steps 2 and 3* to string Row 2 and Row 3, threading cord through center beads before reversing order of bead row. When working Row 2, wrap cord around spring bar between gold beads.

A Memory COLLAGE

If that wonderful guy in your life is like most men, he probably has a drawer full of old memories. Gather some of his cherished mementos and arrange them in a framed collage that will proudly hang in his office or den. Look for mementos thin enough to fit between glass and frame back, or purchase a thicker shadow box frame.

1 *Preparation:* Center fabric on foam core, leaving 4" (10 cm) on each side. Adhere fabric to foam core with white glue and tape excess fabric to back.

2 *Layout:* Lay frame on work surface and arrange the mementos within. Place flat items such as photographs and paper items on the bottom layer. Transfer items to the foam core, beginning with the bottom layer; glue or staple to secure. Make sure staples will be covered by the next layer and that all items are 1/4" (6 mm) from edge of board.

3 *Gluing:* For thicker mementos, push gently into the foam core; use silicone or hot glue to hold in place. Apply glue to pins on items with pin backs and push into foam core. Use only glue to secure the top layer. Let dry overnight. Insert into frame, and finish as desired.

LIST of MATERIALS

* Assorted small mementos of choice, size to fit frame depth
* Mini print fabric, 13" x 16" (33 x 40.5 cm)
* 9" x 12" (23 x 30.5 cm) frame
* 1/4" (6 mm) archival quality foam core, 9" x 12" (23 x 30.5 cm)
* White craft glue or silicone glue
* Hot glue gun
* Miscellaneous items: stapler, masking tape

WALL FRAME

Ribbon wall frames are a quick and easy way to display collections in any room. All you need is a tape measure, upholstery tacks and some ribbon. In addition, they give character to a plain wall, creating the illusion of architectural details at a fraction of the cost.

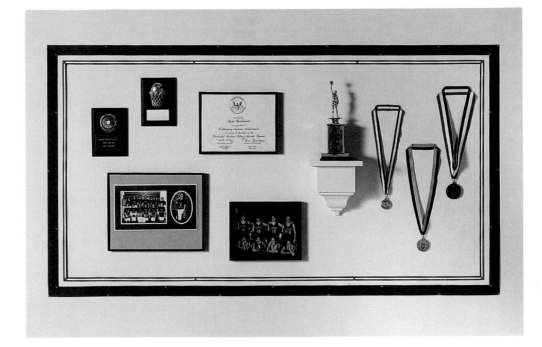

1 *Plan:* Measure the wall accurately; draw to scale on a piece of graph paper. Include any windows, doors, fixtures or outlets on your plan. Draw ribbon frame to desired size and placement on the plan; include all measurements. Cut a continuous piece of ribbon that will go all around the ribbon frame, plus 3" (7.5 cm).

2 *Wall Preparation:* Remove any hanging items from the walls; wash down walls with a damp rag. Lightly mark with pencil on the walls the placement of the ribbon frame corners, using the graph paper plan.

3 *Wall Frame:* Fold under 1 end of the ribbon 1" (2.5 cm). Align the outer corner of the fold to a marked frame corner; tape ribbon to the wall. Pull the ribbon taut to the next marked corner. See the illustration to miter the ribbon so the point aligns with that corner mark. Hold miter in place with at least 2 upholstery tacks.

LIST of MATERIALS

* Tape measure
* Graph paper and pencil
* Decorative upholstery tacks, hammer
* Ribbon in desired width, for yardage see Step 1
* Miscellaneous items: scissors, masking tape

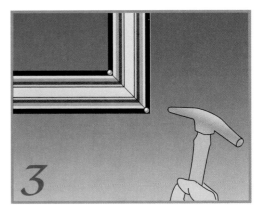

4 *Finishing:* Repeat Step 3 for the next 2 corners. At last corner, diagonally fold ribbon back to create half a miter. Trim excess, and place over beginning point of ribbon. Remove tape, and tack in place. Tack ribbon to wall along ribbon edges; space as desired using tape measure.

Dress up plain wooden pieces with paint and cutouts. No fine art is necessary here; choose your own colors, or follow our design. These homey knickknacks prove that the picket fence doesn't always have to be white and the door is always open, even at night.

LIST of MATERIALS

For Both Projects
* Paintbrushes: ¾" (2 cm) sponge brush, liner brush or fine-line permanent marker, small flat artist's brush
* Hot-glue gun, wood glue

For Screen Door
* 1 unpainted wooden screen door, 7¾" x 17" (19.9 x 43 cm)*
* 1 unpainted wooden moon cutout, 3½" (9 cm)*
* 5 each 1¼" (3.2 cm) and 1½" (3.8 cm) unpainted wooden birdhouse cutouts*
* Acrylic craft paints: turquoise, brown, cream, pink, olive green, black
* Small checkerboard stencil

For Picket Fence
* 1 unpainted wooden picket fence, 10½" x 21½" (26.8 x 54.8 cm)*
* 12 unpainted wooden maple leaf cutouts, 1¼" (3.2 cm)*
* 3 each 1¼" (3.2 cm) and 1½" (3.8 cm) wooden pumpkin cutouts
* Acrylic craft paints: rust, med. brown, dk. brown, orange, burnt sienna, black, green, yellow, red
* Miscellaneous items: paint palette, fine sandpaper
* (See Sources on pg. 159 for purchasing information.)

SCREEN DOOR

1 *Screen Door:* Refer to page 156 for Painting Instructions and Techniques. Refer to photo to basecoat outer frame with ¾" (2 cm) sponge brush and turquoise paint. Basecoat inner frame with brown and door handle cream. Let dry and lightly sand outer edges of door frame for a distressed, worn look.

2 *Border:* Refer to photo to use checkerboard stencil to make the border with brown paint along the turquoise frame. Let dry, then use end of artist's brush handle to make a cream dot in the center of each brown square.

3 *Moon:* Basecoat moon with cream paint; let dry. Use wood glue to adhere moon to upper left corner of inner door frame; refer to photo for placement.

4 *Birdhouses:* Basecoat 3 birdhouses with cream, 2 with turquoise, 2 with pink and 3 with olive green. Paint sizes in color of your choice, or refer to photo. Let dry. Use liner brush and black paint or marker to outline top of birdhouse along roofline. Refer to illustration to hot-glue birdhouses to screen.

PICKET FENCE

1 *Fence:* Refer to page 156 for Painting Instructions and Techniques. Refer to photo to basecoat fence lightly with ¾" (2 cm) sponge brush and rust paint. Streak with medium and dark brown.

2 *Pumpkins:* Basecoat pumpkins with orange; shade with burnt sienna. See illustration to use marker to draw pumpkin faces or paint with liner brush and black paint. Paint leaves and stems with green and brown on 3 smaller pumpkins. Refer to photo to adhere pumpkins to fence with wood glue, placing 2 smaller pumpkins on tallest fence posts.

3 *Leaves:* Dab orange, green, red, yellow and rust paint onto leaves with sponge brush in a random manner. Glue leaves onto fence with wood glue as shown in photo.

ountry Candle
COLLECTION

Make an entire collection

of candles with rustic trims. They are easily made by rolling sheets of beeswax around a wick, not at all like the laborious process of candle dipping. Use your homemade candles in the bath, living room or anywhere you want to set a tranquil scene.

LIST of MATERIALS

For Each Candle
* Beeswax sheets: two 6½" x 16" (16.3 x 40.5 cm) natural, for sunflower candle; three 5½" x 16" (14 x 40.5 cm) burgundy, for twig candle; 4" x 8" (10 x 20.5 cm) sheets, one each burgundy, natural, cinnamon, for candle trio
* 2/0 square braid candlewick, ½ yd. (0.5 m)
* Natural raffia for sunflower and candle trio
* Hot glue gun

For Sunflower Candle
* Natural burlap, 3½" x 8" (9 x 20.5 cm)
* Small silk sunflower

For Twig Candle
* 4" (10 cm) pre-tied twigs, 9" (23 cm) length
* Burlap, 2" (5 cm) squares, one each: green, natural
* 7 assorted coordinating buttons

For Candle Trio
* Gold paper, 2½" x 8" (6.5 x 20.5 cm)
* Sunflower rubber stamp
* Brown stamp pad
* Paint tube wringer (optional)
* Miscellaneous items: scissors, craft knife, ruler, heavy natural thread, sewing needle, stove, metal pie plate

1 *Caution:* Always remove decorative trim before burning candle. Never leave a burning candle unattended.

2 *Making Candles:* Cut wax sheets with craft knife to dimensions in List of Materials. Place wick widthwise across short end of wax sheet $1/8$" (3 mm) in from end. Leave $1/4$" (6 mm) extending at bottom and $3/4$" (2 cm) extending at top. Roll edge of sheet over wick; press firmly, embedding wick in beeswax. Use palm of hand to roll beeswax, keeping an even pressure along candle length. To add additional sheets, see Step 2 illustration. Slightly overlap ends about $1/8$" (3 mm) and press firmly to join. Continue to roll; gently press outer edge along candle to seal.

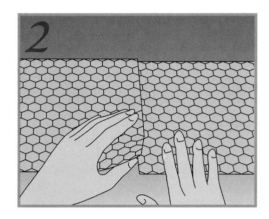

3 *Finishing Candle:* Set candle on end on flat work surface. If it is level, proceed with decorating. If not, heat a metal pie plate on stovetop burner. Place candle bottom on heated pie plate; this melts the wax, leveling the candle and sealing the wick.

4 *Sunflower Candle:* Refer to Steps 2 and 3 to make candle from 2 natural sheets. Place candle on flat surface, seam down, and press firmly and evenly to make an oval-shaped candle. Wrap burlap around candle. Overlap ends at back; hot-glue. Tie raffia around burlap; knot and trim. Hot-glue sunflower to raffia knot.

5 *Twig Candle:* Refer to Steps 2 and 3 to make candle from 3 burgundy sheets. Hot-glue twigs around candle; glue at back. Stitch heavy thread through button holes. Refer to the photo to hot-glue burlap and buttons to twigs.

6 *Candle Trio:* Refer to Steps 2 and 3 to make 3 candles, 1 from each sheet of wax. Cluster candles together with seams inside. Use brown stamp pad and sunflower rubber stamp to decorate gold paper. If desired, run paper through tube wringer for corrugated look. Wrap paper around candle set; overlap and glue ends at back. Tie raffia around center of paper; knot and trim.

Decoupage DINNERWARE

***W*hen the mood strikes** to put together a seasonal table setting, don't head to the department store for expensive dinnerware. Instead, check out the fabric store! Purchase clear glass plates, then use a simple liquid finish to decoupage decorator print fabrics onto the backs of the plates.

LIST of MATERIALS

* 10" (25.5 cm) glass plate
* Fabric, your choice, 13" (33 cm) square
* Laminating finish or decoupage glue
* 1" (2.5 cm) sponge brush
* Miscellaneous items: scissors, plastic garbage bag, large plastic bowl

TIPS and IDEAS

❋ Use coordinating fabric to make a tablecloth, placemats and napkins.

❋ Make a set of dishes for each holiday or season.

1 *Wash and dry fabric* to remove sizing. Do not use fabric softener. Clean plate well with glass cleaner or vinegar.

2 *Work in a well-ventilated area.* Cover work surface with plastic bag. Slide plastic bowl inside bag to center. Position plate facedown on plastic-covered bowl. Brush a generous coat of finish or glue onto back of plate; see Step 2 illustration.

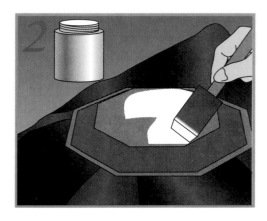

3 *Place fabric right side down* on wet surface. Smooth fabric with brush from center of plate to edges to release air bubbles. Apply more finish as necessary during smoothing to saturate the fabric, as shown in the illustration.

4 *While wet, pull fabric tight* and trim excess fabric from plate edge; see the Step 4 illustration. Apply another coat of finish, making sure fabric edges are bonded to plate. Let dry according to manufacturer's instructions.

5 *Apply final coat of finish.* Let dry 24 hours. Hand wash decoupaged dinnerware; do not place in dishwasher.

Lingerie SILHOUETTES

Transform lingerie

from ordinary to luxurious when you add your own personal touch of glamour. These lovely appliqué ladies, complete with feathers, will tickle the fancy of someone you love. A perfect shower or birthday gift!

LIST of MATERIALS

* Lingerie of your choice: robe, camisole, tap pants, nightgown, etc.
* Black iron-on silhouette appliqués, one for each lingerie piece
* Miscellaneous items: iron, pressing cloth

1 *Wash garment* and lightly press to remove wrinkles. Gently peel paper backing from back of silhouette. Position silhouette in desired location, fusible side down, before adhering to garment; see the illustration.

2 *Follow manufacturer's instructions* for fusing. Test all edges; repeat process if necessary. Let cool. To launder, turn garment inside out, and place in lingerie bag.

TIPS and IDEAS

* You could make your own silhouettes from fabric and fusible web.

Tie DAZZLERS

The perfect accessory for his or her wardrobe—a decorated tie! Embellish a man's necktie for a much-appreciated handcrafted gift. Use these two versions as a springboard to make one suited to the individual's style.

LIST of MATERIALS

For Each Tie
* Man's necktie, your color and design choice
* Jewelry glue
* Needlenose pliers
* Toothpicks

For Rhinestone Tie
* Crystal rhinestones: 3 mm, 13; 8 mm, three

For Rosebud Tie
* ½" (1.3 cm) ribbon roses with leaves to match necktie, 11
* Pearls, 30 assorted: 2 mm, 2.5 mm, 3 mm
* Fabric paint, color to coordinate with tie

1 *Rosebud Tie:* Refer to the photo and arrange roses in clusters of 3 or 4. Apply dabs of glue with toothpick to the tie and press roses in place. Paint additional leaves and dots around roses. Press pearls into wet paint. Also glue pearls onto flowers. Let tie dry overnight before wearing.

2 *Rhinestone Tie:* Refer to the photo and arrange stones as desired on tie. Lift each stone with pliers. See illustration to apply a dab of glue with toothpick to the tie and press stone in place. Let tie dry overnight before wearing.

TIPS and IDEAS

* Buy a solid-colored tie and paint on swaths of favorite colors to look like the purchased tie decorated with rhinestones.
* Make a design with fabric paint and embellishments using the tie recipient's name or favorite hobby.

You can cover a weary old frame or dollar-store find and turn it into something wonderful. The glitzy glass and star charms are perfect for children's photos, and the natural beauty of the drieds works for outdoor scenes as well as more sentimental moments.

For Flower Frame
* Flat wood picture frame
* Dried florals: natural gypsophila, 2-oz. (60 g) package; green gypsophila, 1-oz. (30 g) package; 12 mauve globe amaranth heads; 8 mauve baby rosebuds
* Hot glue gun
* Scissors

For Beaded Frame
* 4½" (11.5 cm) square black wood photo frame with 2" (5 cm) square opening
* Assorted glass beads: seed, rocaille, E-beads, bugle
* ⅜" to ¾" (1 to 2 cm) assorted brass star charms, eight
* Clear silicone glue
* Miscellaneous items: paper towels, shoe-box lid, tweezers, craft stick

FLOWER FRAME

1 Cut or break natural gypsophila into 1" (2.5 cm) pieces. Gather in clusters large enough to cover width of frame. Beginning at 1 corner, hot-glue stems together and then to frame front. Continue to glue clusters overlapping previous stems until entire frame is covered.

2 See the Step 2 illustration to hot-glue 3 globe amaranth in a cluster in each frame corner. Break green gypsophila into 1" (2.5 cm) clusters and glue to each side of globe amaranth.

3 Hot-glue 2 rosebuds at center of each frame side.

BEADED FRAME

1 Remove backing and glass from frame and wipe frame clean with damp paper towels.

2 Working over box lid, spread glue onto frame front a small area at a time and sprinkle with beads. See Step 2 illustration. Repeat until entire front of frame is covered. Let dry 24 hours.

3 Fill in any blank areas with beads. Glue star charms randomly onto frame. Let dry 24 hours. Replace glass and backing.

*N*othing could be easier than making a birdbath from a terra-cotta pot and saucer. Except for maybe making the cute bows and sunflowers. No, you don't have to be an artist at all— the designs are foolproof rub-on transfers that can withstand the elements while filling your backyard with feathered friends.

LIST of MATERIALS

* 5" (12.5 cm) terra-cotta pot
* 8" (20.5 cm) terra-cotta saucer
* Sunflower and Blue Bow rub-on transfers*
* Acrylic craft paint or ceramic paint: cream, yellow
* Paint designed for exterior use:* cream, yellow

* Extra-thick clear finish acrylic spray or exterior-use clear coat*
* 1" (2.5 cm) paintbrush
* Miscellaneous items: very fine sandpaper, measuring tape

*(See Sources on pg. 159 for purchasing information.)

1 *Preparation:* Lightly sand any rough spots. Wash pot and saucer with warm water only; let dry. Do not use any detergent or glass cleaners. Apply 2-3 coats of extra-thick clear finish to all surfaces and let dry.

2 *Painting:* Apply 2-3 coats of each paint with paintbrush to cover thoroughly. Let dry completely between each coat and before applying transfers. Refer to the Step 2 illustration and the photo to paint as follows: the saucer cream on the inside and rim, and yellow on the bottom and side below rim; the pot rim cream, and the pot bottom and side below rim yellow.

3 *Pot:* Follow the manufacturer's instructions to apply the transfers as described below. See the Step 3 illustration to turn the pot upside down and position the sunflower design along the pot rim.

4 *Saucer:* Apply the sunflower bonnet design on the inside center of the saucer. Apply the bow border, spacing as desired, along inner rim of saucer. Peel off the backing paper after recommended length of time, to reveal the transfer as shown in the Step 4 illustration.

5 *Finishing:* Allow transfers to cure 48 hours, or recommended length of time. Apply 3 coats of extra-thick clear finish to all surfaces, following manufacturer's instructions for drying times between coats. Set clay saucer on top of upside-down pot as shown in photo.

Treasure Box
FOR DAD

Dad will be king more than a day when presented with this elegant plaid box. It's just the right size to hold jewelry or other treasures.

LIST of MATERIALS

❊ 7-mesh plastic canvas, 1½ sheets
❊ Worsted knitting yarn: 55 yd. (50.6 m) red; 32 yd. (29.4 m) black
❊ 12 yd. (11.04 m) gold metallic ribbon, ⅛" (3 mm)
❊ No. 16 tapestry needle
❊ 9" x 12" (23 x 30.5 cm) double-sided adhesive sheets, two
❊ 9" x 12" (23 x 30.5 cm) felt sheets, one each: black, red
❊ Pattern Sheet
❊ Miscellaneous items: Marking pen, scissors or craft knife

1 *Cutting:* Refer to the charts on the pattern sheet to cut the lid top, ends and sides from plastic canvas. Also cut one 50x32-bar piece for the box bottom, two 50x14-bar pieces for the box sides and two 32x14-bar pieces for the box ends. Cut up to, but not into, the edge bars.

2 *Box Sides & Ends:* Refer to the Plastic Canvas General Instructions and Stitches on page 158. Work in red slanting Gobelin stitches.

3 *Lid Top, Sides & End Pieces:* Work each piece in continental stitches, beginning with the crown, then the crown background and the gold border. Fill in unmarked areas on chart with red stitches.

4 *Box Assembly:* Use black yarn to overcast the lid sides to the lid top, lid sides together at corners, and along bottom edge. With red yarn, overcast the unstitched box bottom to the box sides and ends, box sides together at corners, and along top edge.

5 *Box Lining:* Cut a 7¼" x 4½" (18.7 x 11.5 cm) piece of black felt for the lid top. From red felt, cut 7" x 4¼" (18 x 10.8 cm) for the box bottom, two 7" x 1¾" (18 x 4.5 cm) pieces for the sides and two 4½" x 1½" (11.5 x 3.8 cm) pieces for the ends. Cut the same from adhesive sheets. Remove backing, and adhere adhesive to canvas, and then press felt in place.

A Stringer OF LURES

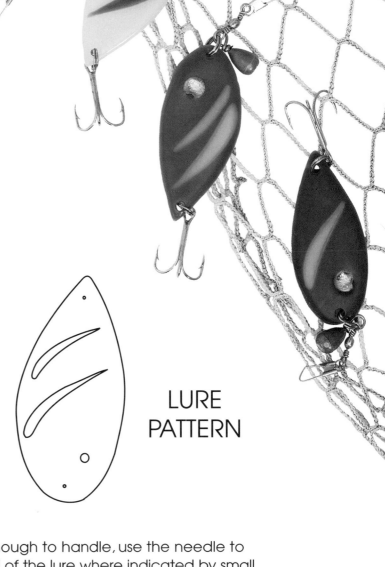

Going fishing for a present? Your favorite angler will fall hook, line and sinker for these great neon lures! An easy-to-shape plastic makes it so-o-o simple to make a stringer of lures in just minutes.

LIST of MATERIALS

* Shrink plastic, one strip each: green, orange, yellow, pink
* 7 mm slip rings, eight
* Size 10 swivel, four
* Size 4 three-prong hook, four
* 7 mm acrylic crystal stones, four
* Miscellaneous items: scissors, pencil, tracing paper, cookie sheet, large darning needle, oven

1 *Pattern:* Trace onto tracing paper and cut out. Trace 1 onto each color of plastic; use scissors to cut out. Refer to the pattern to cut contrasting color pieces to represent fins.

2 *Baking:* Heat oven to 350°F (180°C). Place lures on cookie sheet. Refer to the pattern to lay 1 or 2 fin pieces on each lure. Place acrylic stone on each head for an eye. Bake for 2 minutes or until fins are melted into lure. Remove from oven and let cool.

LURE
PATTERN

3 *Assembly:* When cool enough to handle, use the needle to make a hole in each end of the lure where indicated by small dots on pattern. Attach slip ring through each hole. Attach swivel to mouth hole of each lure, and hook to tail end.

Ruffled Ribbon
JEWELRY

*U*nusual, to say the least, but never easier. This jewelry is created with polypropylene ribbon, available in many textures. When touched with hot glue, this ribbon ruffles, bends, curves, twists, shrinks and melts.

LIST of MATERIALS

* 1 yd. (0.95 m) each gold polypropylene ribbon, 1¼" (3.2 cm) wide: glitter, metallic tone, nouveau moiré
* Acrylic gemstones, bright colors: 15 mm round, 10 x 14 mm oval, 13 x 18 mm oval; 1 for earrings or pin, 3 for pendant
* Crystal glitter dimensional paint writer
* Hot glue gun
* Earring post and disc for pin or earrings
* Rattail cord for pendant chain
* Miscellaneous items: scissors, aluminum foil

1 *Caution:* Glue must be very hot for this technique. Hot glue can burn your skin, so exercise caution when using. After you have glued 2 pieces, let glue gun reheat.

2 *Practicing:* Practice with short pieces of ribbon until comfortable with ribbon ruffling. The more glue you apply to the ribbon, the more it will shrink; but heavy gluing may melt through thinner ribbon.

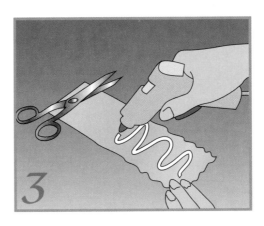

3 *Ruffling Ribbon:* Cover work area with aluminum foil and place ribbon vertically facedown on foil. Weight the top end of ribbon with a heavy object. Hold glue gun in 1 hand and bottom end of ribbon with other hand. Slowly apply hot glue to ribbon in a zigzag motion, as shown in Step 3 illustration. Ribbon will immediately begin to curl. Remove the weight and squeeze glue to top end, letting ribbon curl onto itself. Let glue cool.

4 *Finishing:* Trim any glue from the right side with scissors. Glued pieces can also be cut into any shape. Use the dimensional paint writer to outline edge of ribbon pieces.

5 *Earrings or Pin:* Cut a 3" to 4" (7.5 to 10 cm) length of 2 different ribbons. Glue a smaller piece of different ribbon to base. Glue oval stone to ribbon. Glue earring post and disc to back of each finished piece.

6 *Pendant:* Glue 2 matching larger pieces together vertically. Add 2 cross pieces on top with 2 smaller pieces layered. Randomly glue 3 stones on ribbon. Center and glue rattail cord to top back of pendant. Knot ends.

Tin Punch
STOOL

*M*ake the geometric design with hammer and nail, then paint the top with a fabulous metallic finish that gives the illusion of pewter. In just minutes, you'll transform an ordinary wood stool into a fashionable furniture item.

LIST of MATERIALS

* Unfinished wood stool with 12" (30.5 cm) diameter seat
* Acrylic paints: slate gray, metallic silver
* 1 pint (500 mL) white latex paint
* Polyurethane finish
* Flat paintbrush

* Hammer
* Large nail
* Pattern Sheet
* Miscellaneous items: tracing paper, pencil, sandpaper, masking tape, tack cloth, paper towels

1 *Trace the pattern* onto tracing paper. Center and tape to stool seat. Use the hammer and nail to punch 1/8" (3 mm) deep holes through the pattern, as shown in illustration.

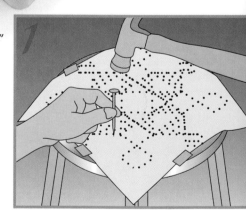

2 *Remove pattern,* sand seat, legs and rungs lightly and wipe with tack cloth. Paint legs and rungs white and let dry.

3 *Refer to page 156* for Painting Instructions and Techniques. Basecoat entire stool seat slate gray, brushing paint into nail holes. Let dry. Drybrush top and sides of seat with metallic silver paint; let dry. Apply finish following manufacturer's instructions; let dry.

Copper
PUNCH CLOCK

This copper punch clock, made with a sheet of copper and some metal punch tools (a nail and a hammer will do) will fit into any country decor.

LIST of MATERIALS

- ❋ .010 copper sheet, 9" (23 cm) square
- ❋ ¼" (6 mm) cork sheet, 9" (23 cm) square
- ❋ Metal punch tools: large, small; or a large and small nail
- ❋ Black acrylic paint
- ❋ 1" (2.5 cm) sponge brush
- ❋ Clear acrylic finish
- ❋ Battery operated clockworks
- ❋ Black clock hands
- ❋ 9" (23 cm) square wood frame
- ❋ Craft cement
- ❋ Pattern Sheet
- ❋ Miscellaneous items: tin snips, tracing paper, pencil, craft knife, ruler, cardboard, masking tape, soft cloth, rubbing alcohol, scissors, hammer

1 Use craft knife to cut a ½" (1.3 cm) circle in center of cork. Use cardboard to spread a thin, even layer of cement on cork. Press copper in place and let dry.

2 Trace the pattern onto tracing paper. Center and tape on copper. Punch through pattern and copper using hammer and large nail or punch for outer ring and intersecting points. Use small nail or punch for remaining holes. To cut out center opening, make small punches close together.

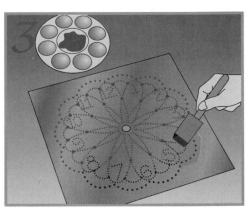

3 See the Step 3 illustration to brush black paint into holes; wipe excess with soft cloth. Clean any remaining paint residue from clock face, using alcohol if necessary. Apply acrylic finish to clock face following manufacturer's instructions; let dry. Insert clockworks and hands; frame as desired.

Summer Cover-Up
& TOTE

Quick, easy and inexpensive describe these lace-trimmed items. They take only a few minutes to make with lace doilies and a liquid adhesive that fuses like web when heated with a dry iron. The results are great and no one will guess that they came right from your ironing board and not the hottest boutique in town!

For Both Projects
* White Battenberg lace medallions and appliqués
* Liquid iron-on adhesive
* Liquid fray preventer

For Tote
* Natural canvas bag

For Summer Cover-Up
* Oversize white cotton or cotton/blend T-shirt
* Miscellaneous items: scissors, iron, press cloth, tea bag, terrycloth towel, craft knife, cardboard to fit in bag or shirt

T-SHIRT

1 Wash and dry T-shirt and appliqués; press to remove wrinkles. Insert cardboard or T-shirt board inside shirt and place on flat surface. Position appliqué on bodice center front carefully, remembering that fabric behind appliqué will be cut out.

2 Follow the manufacturer's instructions to heat iron. On wrong side, squeeze a thin line of liquid adhesive around edge of appliqué as shown in the illustration. Place appliqué, adhesive side down, on shirt front; cover with press cloth and press edges for recommended time. Remove cloth and let cool.

3 Test adherence of appliqué by gently lifting edges. If not secure, apply adhesive under edge and repeat pressing. If adhesive seeps out from under edge, remove from fabric by dabbing with a wet cloth. Avoid excessive pressing, which may scorch the fabric and appliqué.

4 From inside, carefully cut out opening in shirt around the inner fused edge of appliqué, making sure not to cut lace. Apply liquid fray preventer to cut edges.

5 Repeat Steps 2-4 to fuse appliqués and cut out openings on sleeves and rest of shirt front.

TOTE

1 If desired, tea-dye lace medallions to match canvas tote. Place a tea bag in 1⅓ cups (325 mL) of boiling water for 3 minutes, stirring occasionally. Remove tea bag. Place lace in tea for 3 minutes, stirring constantly. Remove lace and rinse in cold running water until water runs clear. Squeeze excess water from lace and blot dry with towel. While still damp, use press cloth to iron lace; lay flat until thoroughly dry.

2 Use a craft knife to cut a piece of heavy cardboard to fit inside bag. Refer to the photo to place lace medallions in desired positions on front of canvas bag, marking placement with pins.

3 See T-Shirt Steps 2-4 to fuse lace medallions to tote, and cut out the canvas tote from behind; see the Step 3 illustration.

Indoor & OUTDOOR BOXES

All it takes to personalize the rough-sided outdoor boxes is rubber stamps and paint; the boxes are even prestained. The more decorative smooth planter boxes with round feet are so versatile, that after painting and decoupaging, you may use them for wastebaskets, towels, magazines and plants. Coordinate with a tissue box as shown, and you have an ensemble for bedroom or bath.

LIST of MATERIALS

For Outdoor Boxes
* 1 each prestained 6" (15 cm) and 9" (23 cm) square planter box*
* Rubber stamps: ferns, leaves, and sun
* Acrylic craft paints: metallic copper, olive green, and forest green, blue

For Indoor Boxes
* 1 wooden planter box with feet (7.4" x 8.6" x 7.4")*
* 1 wooden tissue box (5 1/8" x 5 1/8" x 6 1/8" (12.8 x 12.8 x 15.4 cm))*
* Decoupage medium
* Wrapping paper with fish or tissue paper with flowers
* Acrylic craft paints: black, metallic gold
* Miscellaneous items: paint palette, fine sandpaper, tack cloth, ruler, pencil, 1" (2.5 cm) sponge brush, scissors

*(See Sources on pg. 159 for purchasing information.)

OUTDOOR BOXES

1 *Painting:* Paint planter box upper edge with desired paints, such as metallic copper on the large box.

2 *Stamping:* Apply paint to stamps with sponge brush. Practice stamping on scrap paper first. Press the rubber stamp firmly and evenly onto box; do not roll the stamp. Apply more paint to the stamp as needed. Lay planter boxes on their sides, and apply rubber stamps randomly as follows: green box with metallic copper suns, olive green leaves and forest green leaves, and blue box with blue, forest green and olive green ferns.

INDOOR BOXES

1 *General:* Lightly sand all surfaces of box; remove dust with tack cloth. Follow manufacturer's instructions to assemble planter box. Refer to page 156 for Painting Instructions and Techniques. Basecoat box, inside and out, with sponge brush and black paint for fish box and metallic gold for flower box. Dry-brush metallic gold paint on the top edge and ball feet. Paint only inside rim of tissue box with gold paint.

2 *Fish Box:* Cut a strip of wrapping paper long enough to go around box; strip may be pieced. Measure from top edge of box to where you would like the strip to begin, and make a few light pencil marks on each side. See Step 2 illustration to place wrapping paper border at the marks, and apply to box with decoupage medium, following manufacturer's instructions. Seal entire outer box with 1 or more coats of medium.

3 *Flower Boxes:* Cut tissue paper to fit each side of box, and tissue box top, adding ⅛" (3 mm) for overlap on all sides of top piece, and sides only of side pieces. Apply decoupage medium to tissue box top, then to 1 side at a time, following manufacturer's instructions. See illustration to carefully adhere tissue to medium. Lightly rub and smooth paper with sponge brush to remove bubbles and wrinkles, before doing next side. Repeat for sides only of planter box.

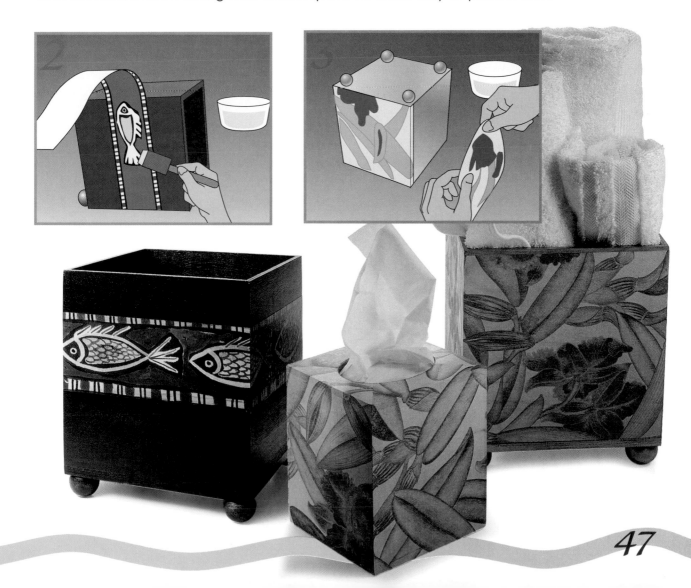

Create fanciful fruits

so tempting you'll want to take a bite! Display a bowl, box or basketful on your table or counter. You can make them in an evening, they cost just pennies, and kids love to help.

❋ Styrofoam® shapes: 3⅞" (9.7 cm) egg for apple or pear, 3" (7.5 cm) ball for orange

❋ Cotton fabrics, colored solids or small prints, ⅛ yd. (0.15 m) for each fruit

❋ 2" (5 cm) cloth rose leaf, one each for apple or pear

❋ 20-gauge floral wire, 6" (15 cm) each for apple or pear

❋ Green floral tape

❋ White craft glue

❋ Miscellaneous items: scissors, ruler, wire cutters, sharp serrated knife

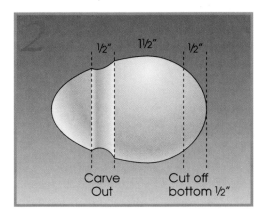

½"   1½"   ½"

Carve Out   Cut off bottom ½"

1 *Shaping Fruit:* Use the serrated knife blade edge to make cuts from Styrofoam. Use your hands to press or roll foam shapes on a hard surface to round and smooth cut edges.

2 *Pear:* See the Step 2 illustration to cut off the bottom and carve a curved indentation around egg.

3 *Apple:* Cut ½" (1.3 cm) off the large end of egg for the top. Cut a ¾" (2 cm) circular indentation around center, similar to the cut for the pear in Step 2 above. Cut ¾" (2 cm) off small end for bottom.

4 *Stem & Leaf:* Fold a 6" (15 cm) length of floral wire in half. If edges of leaf are jagged, trim to make a smooth-edged leaf. Position leaf ¾" (2 cm) from wire fold and tightly wrap with floral tape. Insert leaf into center top of apple or pear to determine position. Remove and set aside.

5 *Fabric Strips:* Cut fabric into ½" (1.3 cm) strips along the fabric width. Make 4 or 5 strips for each fruit. If fabric ravels slightly, this only adds to its charm. See illustration to glue end of a fabric strip to fruit shape and wrap vertically, diagonally and horizontally around fruit; glue other end.

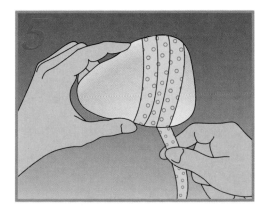

6 *Finishing:* Repeat to wrap and completely cover fruit. Do not cover leaf hole of apple or pear. For the apple, apply small amount of glue to strips as you wrap to build up around top indentation. Coat leaf stem with glue and insert into apple or pear.

Pretty and practical are these richly, but quickly, embellished towel ensembles. The rose is cross-stitched onto premade Aida ovals, complete with eyelet edging. All you have to do after stitching is fuse the ovals onto the towels.

LIST of MATERIALS

* Towels of your choice, one each: bath, hand, washcloth
* Ivory Aida ovals: 14-count, 4" x 5" (10 x 12.5 cm), two; 18-count, 2¾" x 3½" (7 x 9 cm), one (See Sources on pg. 159 for purchasing information.)
* Anchor 6-strand embroidery floss listed on Color Key, 1 skein each
* No. 24 tapestry needle
* Fusible web, 9" x 10" (23 x 25.5 cm)
* Miscellaneous items: scissors, press cloth, iron

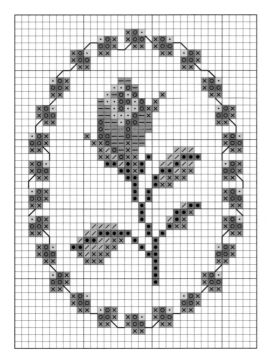

1 *Stitching:* Refer to page 155 for Cross-Stitch Instructions and Stitches. Use the chart to stitch the designs. Stitch large oval with 2 strands of floss. Backstitch the vines with 1 strand of Dk. Juniper 218. Center and stitch only the rose on small oval.

2 *Finishing:* Follow manufacturer's instructions to apply fusible web to back of stitched ovals; see illustration. Center large ovals on 1 end of towels; use press cloth and iron to fuse. Fuse small oval to 1 corner of washcloth.

COLOR KEY

Symbol	Name	Anchor	Symbol	Name	Anchor
•	Very Light Antique Rose	74	╱	Light Juniper	214
—	Medium Antique Rose	76	✕	Medium Juniper	216
⊙	Dark Antique Rose	978	⬤	Dark Juniper	218

Faux-Stone Candleholders
& BEADED BOBÈCHES

For a contemporary table setting, try making these easy candleholders. Because the stone finish covers all, the candleholders can be yard sale finds, and because the finish comes out of a can, you can convert another's junk to your treasure in a very short time. The bobèches, which are designed to catch wax drippings from the candles, need only needlenose pliers and beads to complete a look of pure elegance.

LIST of MATERIALS

For Candleholders
* Pair of wooden candleholders
* Two brass candle inserts*
* Faux-stone finish: charcoal sand*
* Acrylic craft paints: gray; Metallics: gold and silver
* 1 small paintbrush
* Painter's masking tape
* Clear acrylic sealer

For Bobèches
* Two glass or acrylic ring cups with holes around outer edges*
* 12 head pins
* Assorted beads, 6 each of 4-5 kinds
* Wire cutters
* Needlenose pliers
* Chain-nose pliers or tweezers
* Miscellaneous items: fine sandpaper, tack cloth

*(See Sources on pg. 159 for purchasing information.)

TIPS and IDEAS

* Some candle shops have ring cups for the bobèches with the loops already attached. All you need to do is bead the pins and insert them into the loops.

CANDLEHOLDERS

1 Preparation: Refer to Painting Instructions and Techniques on pg. 156. Lightly sand candleholders; wipe away dust with tack cloth. Basecoat candleholders with gray paint; let dry. Cut painter's masking tape to fit around areas where you want to paint metallic bands; pinch together tape around curves.

2 Stone Finish: Apply as shown in the Step 2 illustration to candleholders following manufacturer's instructions. Apply desired number of coats; let dry between coats as recommended by manufacturer.

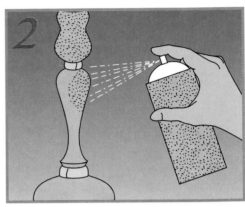

3 Finishing: Remove tape. Mix 1 part gold paint with 1 part silver paint. Paint contrasting bands; let dry. Apply sealer to candleholders, following manufacturer's instructions. Tap brass candle inserts into top of candleholders.

BOBÈCHES

1 Ring Cup Loops: Put a head pin into a hole in ring cup from top side. Cut pin to 3/4" (2 cm) with wire cutters. Insert end of pin into needlenose pliers jaws. See illustration to roll pliers, coiling wire up to ring cup. Repeat for other 5 holes around ring cup.

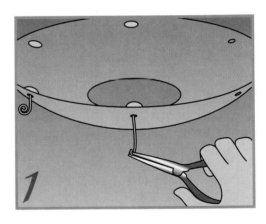

2 Beaded Drops: Place your choice of beads on another head pin in desired order, beginning with a small hole bead. Cut head pin at last bead, leaving 3/8" (1 cm). Bend wire at 90° angle just above last bead. Insert end of head pin into jaws of needlenose pliers. Roll until end meets head pin, making a round loop. Repeat to make 6 beaded drops.

3 Finishing: Open round loop at end of beaded drop by grasping one half of loop in tweezers or the jaws of chain-nose pliers and rotating it away from you. Do not pull loop apart to open or you will distort the nice round loop shape. Slip beaded drop loop into loop hanging on ring cup as shown in the Step 3 illustration. Close loop in same manner as it was opened. Repeat for each beaded drop.

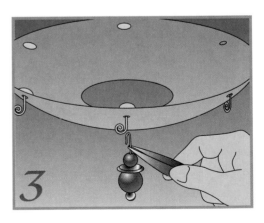

Yo Yo Placemats
& NAPKIN RINGS

The making of yo yos has almost become a lost art. Today, because premade yo yos are widely available, you can enjoy the fun of creating with these puffy circles without the tedious work.

LIST of MATERIALS

* Woven placemat and napkin
* ⅔ yd. (0.63 m) coordinating ⅜" (1 cm) satin ribbon
* Premade yo yos: 13 large (1½" (3.8 cm)), 5 small (1⅛" (2.8 cm)) (See Sources on pg. 159 for purchasing information.)
* Miscellaneous items: Washable fabric glue, straight pins

1 **Yo Yos:** If you prefer to make your own yo yos to better coordinate with your decor, see page 158 for instructions.

2 **Placemat:** Refer to the photo to arrange large yo yos along 1 short edge of placemat. Overlap slightly and glue in place, as shown in Step 2 illustration.

3 **Napkin Ring:** See illustration to glue 1 small yo yo at ribbon center. Glue 2 overlapping yo yos on either side. When dry, tie around rolled napkin.

Honeycomb NAPKIN RINGS

Strips of honeycomb paper glued and woven through with raffia tied in a bow make superfast napkin rings for contemporary or casual entertaining.

LIST of MATERIALS

* Brown paper honeycomb sheets (See Sources on pg. 159 for purchasing information.)
* Natural raffia
* Low-temp glue gun
* Scissors

1 *Refer to manufacturer's instructions* to cut a piece of honeycomb 4 diamonds (2" (5 cm)) high and 20 diamonds wide.

2 *Hot-glue straight edges* of honeycomb strip together to form a ring. Weave 2 to 3 strands of raffia over and under every other diamond all the way around the center of the ring, as shown in the illustration. Tie raffia ends into a bow.

Decoupaged LUGGAGE

Search your attic or basement for that abandoned hard-sided
luggage and give it new life with decoupage. Victorian wrapping paper or
memorabilia items cover up any scars to create an elegant look. Use your
refurbished luggage as a decorating showpiece, or for its original purpose,
as a traveling companion.

* 3/4" (2 cm) sponge brush
* Decoupage glue or double-sided sheet adhesive
* Hard-sided luggage
* Victorian wrapping paper, memorabilia, doilies, etc.
* Waterbased varnish or lacquer (optional)
* Miscellaneous items: tracing paper, pencil, scissors, leather cleaner or mild soap and water, soft cloth, craft knife

1 *Preparation:* Wash the outside of the luggage with a leather cleaner or mild soap and water. Let dry.

2 *Wrapping Paper:* Trace a pattern of the luggage using paper and pencil. Cut the pattern from the wrapping paper, making the pieces slightly larger than the original.

3 *Gluing:* Use decoupage glue or sheet adhesive to glue the wrapping paper to the luggage. Glue is easier to work with on large areas where the paper may have to be repositioned. See Step 3 illustration to apply glue to the luggage a few inches at a time before pressing the paper in place. Sheet adhesive works well in small areas. Follow the manufacturer's instructions to apply sheet adhesive to the paper. Remove paper backing and press in place on the luggage.

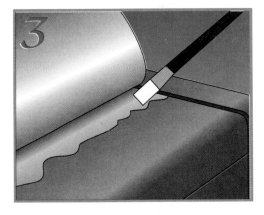

4 *Smoothing & Trimming:* Rub the paper with a soft cloth to remove any air bubbles or excess glue. Using the craft knife, trim any excess paper from around the handles, latches and edges.

5 *Finishing:* Plan where to place the items on the luggage. Adhere with glue or adhesive as in Steps 3 and 4. Follow manufacturer's instructions to apply several coats of the decoupage glue or a waterbase varnish or lacquer to seal the luggage.

*A*utumn WREATH

*W*hen the season turns from summer to fall and the leaves on the trees start their wonderful show, we look for ways to decorate our homes in the golden colors of autumn. This heart wreath preserves summer's bounty, bringing the natural beauty and fragrance of your herb and flower garden indoors.

* Dried sweet Annie or silver king herbs for wreath base, 5 oz. (150 g)
* Dired herbs and flowers for filler, three to five varieties: celosia, yarrow, larkspur, statice, salvia, globe amaranth, rosebuds, poppy pods
* 7/8" (2.2 cm) fall print ribbon, 1¼ yds. (1.15 m)
* Wire: 16-gauge soft hardware, 32" (81.5 cm); 22-gauge paddle
* Hot glue gun or white craft glue
* Miscellaneous items: wire cutters, scissors, ruler, mist spray bottle

1 *Heart Frame:* See the Step 1 illustration to bend 16-gauge wire and make a heart about 8" (20.5 cm) wide by 8" (20.5 cm) high. Use paddle wire to wrap ends; do not cut wire, but leave it connected.

2 *Wreath Base:* Ten minutes before working with the dried herbs and flowers, mist with water for easier handling. Break herbs into 3" (7.5 cm) stems. Group stems into 2" to 3" (5 to 7.5 cm) wide clusters.

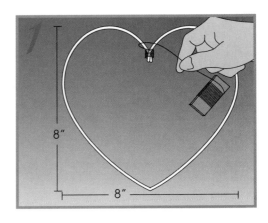

3 *Assembly:* Starting at center top of heart, see the Step 3 illustration to place 1 cluster on wire frame with cluster pointing downward. Wrap wire ½" (1.3 cm) from stem ends 3 times around frame. Place next herb cluster on wire frame overlapping 1" (2.5 cm). Continue layering the herbs, working around and covering the entire wreath. Tuck stems of last cluster under full ends of first cluster. Trim excess wire.

4 *Ribbon:* Make a multi-loop bow with 4" (10 cm) streamers. Cut ends at an angle. Wire bow to center top of heart, bringing wire ends to back and bending to form hanger loop.

5 *Finishing:* Refer to the photo to spot-glue bow loops and streamers on wreath. Glue filler flowers and herbs in a zigzag pattern, starting with the largest materials and ending with the smallest.

Tortoiseshell
FINISH

You can add a new finish to your repertoire with this simple-to-do tortoiseshell technique. Isopropyl alcohol is the key. Dropped over a black paint wash, the alcohol allows the metallic paint underneath it all to come shining through. The result is a rich finish achieved with just a small investment in time!

LIST of MATERIALS

* ⁕ Tilt-top table
* ⁕ Acrylic paints: black; Metallics: gold, bronze, antique gold
* ⁕ High-gloss sealer
* ⁕ 3/4" (2 cm) flat paintbrush
* ⁕ Isopropyl alcohol
* ⁕ Eyedropper
* ⁕ Natural sea sponge
* ⁕ Miscellaneous items: aluminum foil, palette knife, water container, small paper cup, sandpaper, tack cloth

1 *General:* Refer to page 156 for Painting Instructions and Techniques. Sand all surfaces lightly and wipe with tack cloth.

2 *Legs & Underside:* Basecoat as shown in Step 2 illustration with black paint; let dry. Accent stand or legs as desired with gold paint. When dry, brush 1 coat of high-gloss sealer over painted areas.

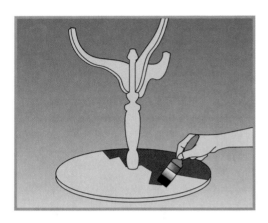

3 *Tabletop Basecoat:* Pour a generous amount of each metallic paint onto aluminum foil. Dip the sponge in gold paint and randomly dab sponge on tabletop; see Step 3 illustration. Rinse the sponge in water and repeat with other 2 metallic paints to cover tabletop. Rinse sponge between each color change. It is not necessary to let colors dry before applying the next color. After all colors have been sponged, let dry.

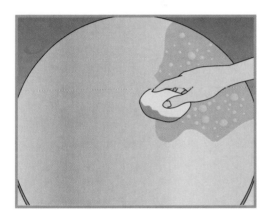

4 *Tortoiseshell Preparation:* Pour a small amount of black paint onto foil. Thin the color with water and a palette knife to a thin wash consistency. Pour 1" (2.5 cm) of isopropyl alcohol in the paper cup.

5 *Tortoiseshell Technique:* Work only with a small area, as the black paint must be wet for the process to work. Brush the black wash onto a small area of the tabletop. See the Step 5 illustration and photo to quickly fill the eyedropper with isopropyl alcohol and gently squeeze different-sized drops of alcohol here and there over the brushed black. The alcohol will cause the black paint to spread apart and reveal the metallic paint underneath.

6 *Finishing:* Repeat Step 5 to complete tabletop; let dry. Brush gold on edge of tabletop. When dry, brush 1 coat of sealer over entire tabletop.

Sunflower Suite
STORAGE

It seems that we all have more stuff than we know what to do with, especially office-type stuff! Buying organizers is all well and good, but they look so sterile and impersonal. Here is a way to decorate cardboard storage products so they look as good as they work. Easy ribbon trimming, stenciling and stamping mean you don't have to spend a lot of time on them, either.

LIST of MATERIALS

For All Storage Items
* Sunflower stencils in various sizes
* Stencil creme paints: green, yellow, brown
* 3 stencil brushes
* Clear acrylic sealer

For 8-Drawer Chest
* Cardboard craft cubby and 8 drawers*

For Magazine File
* Cardboard magazine file*
* 15" (38 cm) sunflower print ribbon or paper ribbon
* Raffia
* Thick white craft glue

For Desktop Organizer
* 4-drawer cardboard supply mate*
* Checkerboard stencil
* Miscellaneous items: ruler, scissors

*(See Sources on pg. 159 for purchasing information.)

ALL ITEMS

Assemble the cardboard storage unit following manufacturer's instructions. Decorate as follows for each individual item. Use green for the sunflower leaves and stems, brown for the sunflower center, and yellow for the sunflower petals. Apply at least 1 coat of acrylic sealer following manufacturer's recommendations.

8-DRAWER CHEST

Stencil the chest top and sides with the entire sunflower border stencil. Use just part of the stencil for decorating the drawers. To shade the sunflower centers, first stencil with yellow, then lightly stencil brown around the edges; see the illustration.

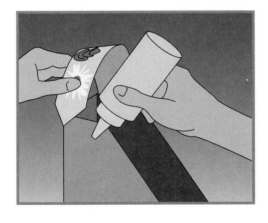

MAGAZINE FILE

Stencil sunflowers on all sides of the magazine file. Cut a 15" (38 cm) strip of sunflower ribbon. Refer to photo to cut ribbon ends in a triangular point. Glue ribbon ends to top center of magazine file as shown in the illustration. Take several strands of raffia, tie them into a bow, and glue to magazine file over ribbon ends.

DESKTOP ORGANIZER

See the illustration to stencil checkerboard design with brown paint on the drawer fronts. Stencil sunflowers on top and sides of the organizer. Randomly blot stencil brush with brown paint around sunflowers.

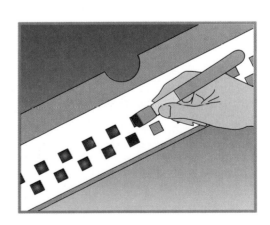

$\mathcal{P}$lacemat PURSES

$\mathcal{P}$lacemats aren't just for tables!

Here are three exciting ways to turn them into designer-style purses. Wouldn't you like to have a purse or tote to match every outfit in your wardrobe? If it sounds wonderful, but terribly expensive, you'll love these easy-to-make designs. Using placemats, the purses are fun to sew, and best of all, very economical!

LIST of MATERIALS

For Straw Tote
* 2 straw octagonal placemats
* 1/8 yd. (0.15 m) coordinating quilted fabric
* 1" (2.5 cm) belting, 1 1/8 yd. (1.05 m)
* Double-fold bias tape, one package

For Reversible Clutch
* Reversible woven rectangular placemat with fringed edges

* 1" (2.5 cm) buttons, two
* 1/4" (6 mm) satin ribbon, 3" (7.5 cm)

For Pleated Purse with Flower
* Pleated octagonal fabric placemat
* 16 1/2" (41.8 cm) matching fabric napkin
* 6" x 12" (15 x 30.5 cm) fusible web
* 30" (76 cm) lightweight gold chain

* 4" (10 cm) hook and loop tape
* Fabric glue
* Pattern Sheet
* Miscellaneous items: sewing machine, iron, scissors, tape measure, tracing paper, pencil, sewing needle, matching threads, straight pins, serger (optional)

STRAW TOTE

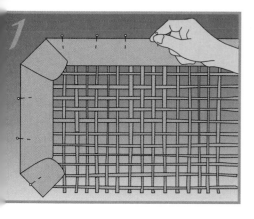

1 *Gusset:* Cut a 4" x 36" (10 x 91.5 cm) strip from quilted fabric. Bind edges with bias tape. Pin-mark gusset centers and each bottom placemat edge. With wrong sides together and matching centers, pin gusset to bottom and side edges of each placemat. See Step 1 illustration; topstitch in place.

2 *Straps:* Cut belting in half. For each strap, turn ends under 1/4" (6 mm) and sew securely to top of placemat, measuring evenly from sides.

REVERSIBLE CLUTCH

1 *Stitching:* Fold bottom short edge of placemat up 7" (18 cm). Sew sides together in a 3/4" (2 cm) seam. Make a loop with ribbon and sew to center of top short edge.

2 *Purse Flap:* Fold top down and mark button placement in center of loop. Sew on button. Turn inside out and sew button on reverse side.

PLEATED PURSE WITH FLOWER

1 *Cutting:* Cut a 2 1/2" x 16 1/2" (6.5 x 41.8 cm) strip from one edge of the napkin and a 2" x 9 1/2" (5 x 24.3 cm) strip from another edge for the flower. Cut a 5" x 5" x 7" (12.5 x 12.5 x 18 cm) triangle from a finished corner for the leaf. Trace the gusset pattern, and cut from napkin and fusible web as indicated.

2 *Gusset:* Use fusible web to fuse 2 pieces with wrong sides together. Satin stitch or serge edges to finish. With right sides together, center and pin each gusset to long placemat edge. Sew a 1/4" (6 mm) seam. Turn and topstitch 1/2" (1.3 cm) at top edge of each gusset seam to reinforce.

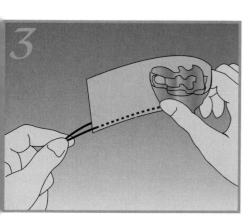

3 *Flower:* Sew a gathering stitch along long raw edge of 2" x 9 1/2" (5 x 24.3 cm) strip. Pull gathering threads tightly as shown in the Step 3 illustration. Turn down 1 finished corner and roll strip to form flower center. Tack bottom edge securely. Gather long raw edge of 16 1/2" (41.8 cm) strip and wrap loosely around center, overlapping ends; tack to center. Gather 7" (18 cm) raw edge of leaf tightly and sew.

4 *Finishing:* Glue or sew flower and leaf to top right purse front. Center and glue hook and loop tape to wrong side of top purse edges. Sew chain ends to wrong side of top front edge.

Magic Erase
MESSAGE BOARD

Make this handy memo board for someone who needs help organizing a hectic schedule. Use your imagination and choose fabric, a novelty gift wrap or cutouts of your favorite photos. The durable iron-on vinyl protecting the board can be written on with a washable marker and wiped off with a tissue. It works great and you'll wonder how you ever got along without one!

LIST of MATERIALS

* 12" x 16" (30.5 x 40.5 cm) mat board
* 15" x 19" (38 x 48.5 cm) gift wrap, fabric, etc.
* Paper-backed fusible web, 1/2 yd. (0.5 m)
* Iron-on clear flexible vinyl, 1/2 yd. (0.5 m)
* Paper cutouts, your choice
* 4 self-adhesive hook and loop fasteners, 1" (2.5 cm) square
* Black permanent marker
* Glue stick
* Miscellaneous items: scissors, ruler, pencil, typing paper, iron

1 Cut a 15" x 19" (38 x 48.5 cm) piece of fusible web. Following the manufacturer's instructions, fuse to the back of gift wrap, photos, fabric, etc. Let cool. Peel off the paper backing and use as a protective surface for your ironing board, glossy side up.

2 Center the fused paper over the mat board, adhesive side down, and iron the mat board area only, not the extending paper edges. Refer to the Step 2 illustration to cut out corners. Fold and iron paper edges, 1 side at a time, tightly around back of the mat board.

Paper-Covered Mat Board Wrong Side Up

3 Write the word "Messages" in the upper left-hand corner of 8" x 10" (20.5 x 25.5 cm) paper with marker. Use glue stick to lightly glue back of paper, and center on front of the mat board. Smooth out air bubbles. Randomly glue paper cutouts, overlapping edge of typing paper as shown in Step 3 illustration. If typing paper is unlined, use pencil and ruler to draw lines.

4 Refer to Step 2 to center and fuse the iron-on vinyl over front of mat board. Adhere one half of hook and loop fasteners on each back corner, the other half to where you want your message board to hang.

New mouse pads with pockets for papers allow you to quickly design and create your own—but best of all, they aren't permanent. Change your mouse-pad artwork, collage or memories every month if you want. With paintbrush and scissors in hand you can add color and shape to regular foam mouse pads; the sky is the limit.

LIST of MATERIALS

For Painted Mouse Pads
* 8" x 9¼" (20.5 x 23.6 cm) mouse pad
* Acrylic craft paints: green and blue for leaf pad, green, blue, red, turquoise and gold for stenciled pad
* Paint tray
* High-density foam roller (approximately 6" x 1⅜" (15 x 3.5 cm) diameter)
* Artist's brushes: small round, ¼" (6 mm) flat
* Aerosol clear acrylic sealer

For Stenciled Mouse Pad
* Stencils in designs of your choice: spirals and squiggles
* Stencil adhesive
* Stencil brush for each color
* Acrylic paint extender

For Artwork Mouse Pad
* Mouse pads designed to hold artwork, calendars, etc.
* Artwork, fabric, pictures, etc. of your choice
* Pattern Sheet (leaf pattern)
* Miscellaneous items: pencil, artist's eraser, scissors, paint palette, paper towels, masking tape, tracing paper

STENCILED MOUSE PAD

1 *Basecoat mouse pad* gold as in Step 1 of Leaf Mouse Pad. Apply stencil adhesive to back of stencil, following manufacturer's instructions. Position stencil on mouse pad as desired.

2 *Mix 2 parts* acrylic craft paint and 1 part acrylic paint extender on paint palette. Dip tip of stencil brush into mixture. Using circular motion, swirl paintbrush onto paper towel until bristles are almost dry. Hold brush perpendicular to surface of stencil; apply paint, using a circular motion.

3 *Paint edge of mouse pad* with acrylic paint, using ¼" (6 mm) flat paintbrush; let dry. Apply a second coat; let dry. Apply clear acrylic sealer to mouse pad, following manufacturer's instructions; let dry.

ARTWORK MOUSE PAD

Mouse pads with protective covers showcase any sort of memorabilia you desire: a favorite drawing from a niece or nephew, a collage of photos, a treasured letter or poem, calendar, piece of favorite fabric or lace. There is no end to what you can display, as long as it is flat.

LEAF MOUSE PAD

1 Squeeze green paint onto paint tray. Run roller through paint to coat evenly. Roll roller over surface of mouse pad to cover with paint. Wrap roller in plastic wrap to keep paint from drying out; let mouse pad dry. Apply second coat; let dry.

2 Trace pattern to tracing paper; cut out. Trace leaf pattern onto front of painted mouse pad with pencil. Cut out leaf shape from mouse pad with scissors. Erase any pencil lines, using an artist's eraser.

3 Paint blue vein lines on leaf, using small round paintbrush; let dry. Refer to pattern and photo for placement. Apply clear acrylic sealer to mouse pad; let dry.

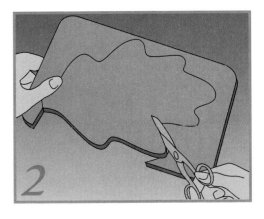

Quicker!

The love and pride you put into a handmade cuddly dinosaur, unique pillow or cherished memory album will make them treasured gifts for special people in your life. They will not,

however, take up all of your spare time. You will still be able to make a floral arrangement, some note cards or a butterfly house for yourself to enjoy as well.

Watercolor
PILLOWS

These gorgeous pillows are so easy to make, you'll want a couchful to snuggle up with! Simply spritz squares of silk fabric with beautiful shades of waterbase spray-on colors. Wrap the painted fabric squares around pillow forms, then add elegant satin ribbon and cord trims for a designer look.

LIST of MATERIALS

* White silk fabric, 36" (91.5 cm) squares, two
* Waterbase spray-on colors: berry, green, gold
* 18" (46 cm) square pillow forms, two
* 1½" (3.8 cm) burgundy/gold satin ribbon, 2 yd. (1.85 m)
* 2 yd. (1.85 m) each satin cord: 12 mm green/gold; 6 mm green
* 6 small round adhesive-backed hook and loop fasteners
* Miscellaneous items: iron, scissors, four 6" (15 cm) yarn lengths, 2 large plastic trash bags, newspaper, rubber band, water container

Wash and press each fabric square. Do not use fabric softener. Place cut-open plastic trash bag on a large flat work surface; protect the surrounding area not covered by plastic with newspapers.

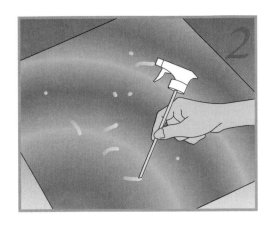

BERRY PILLOW

1 Lay fabric square in the center of the covered work surface. Refer to the manufacturer's instructions to spray the fabric with berry, creating light and dark areas. Dip fingers in clear water and lightly shake them over the fabric, spattering to create water-color spots.

2 Remove pump from the gold spray bottle. Use the tube end of the pump to spatter the fabric with drops of gold color. Randomly wipe the tube across the fabric to create streaks, as shown in illustration. Insert and remove the pump for more paint as needed. Let the fabric dry completely; press.

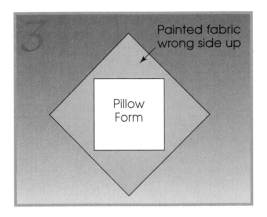

Painted fabric wrong side up

Pillow Form

3 See the Step 3 illustration to position the pillow form on wrong side of fabric. Bring the 4 corners of the fabric together in the center. Hold the corners with 1 hand; wrap them with a rubber band to secure. Arrange soft folds neatly around the pillow top. Tuck the fabric corner ends into the center hole created by the rubber band to form a pouf.

4 Tuck 1 end of the burgundy/gold satin ribbon into the rubber band under the pouf. Wrap the ribbon around the pillow, back to the center front, around the pouf, then repeat around the pillow in the opposite direction. Trim the ribbon end if necessary and tuck it under the rubber band to secure.

GREEN PILLOW

1 See the Step 1 illustration to gather a fabric square from 1 side to the other. Use the 6" (15 cm) yarn lengths to tie off the fabric into 5 even segments. Repeat Step 1 of Berry Pillow to spray the gathered fabric with green, turning it to cover all sides. Let dry. Remove the yarn and lay the fabric out flat. Spray the entire square lightly with green again.

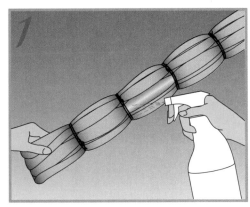

2 Working in the opposite direction, repeat Step 1 of Green Pillow using gold. Repeat Step 2 of Berry Pillow to add gold highlights.

3 Lay pillow as shown in Step 3 of Berry Pillow. Fold the bottom corner of the fabric up over the pillow. Fold over each side corner, then fold down the top corner. Use the adhesive-backed hook and loop fasteners to secure the fabric.

4 Holding the 12 mm and 6 mm cords together, wrap them around the pillow from corner to corner, and knot. Knot the 6 mm cord ends. Tie an overhand knot 4" (10 cm) from the end of each 12 mm cord; unravel the cord ends to form tassels.

Here is a unique way to store precious photos and papers. The document box will work to tuck mail, papers, recipes or memorabilia out of the way. It is easily done with a coat of paint and some rubber stamps. The decoupaged or painted memory book covers will make any album look as marvelous on the outside as it does on the inside.

LIST of MATERIALS

For Document Box
* 1 wooden document box (12³/₄" x 4¹/₂ x 10" (32.4 x 11.5 x 25.5 cm))*
* Rubber stamps: spiral, horses and starbursts*
* Acrylic craft paints: turquoise, blue, copper, gold
* Stencil brush or sponge
* Embossing liquid*
* Embossing powders*: turquoise, black, copper, peach
* Heat gun or other heat source

For Decoupaged Album Cover
* 1 unpainted wooden album cover (6" x 9" (15 x 23 cm))*
* Acrylic craft paints: metallic gold, off-white
* Crackle and decoupage medium
* Leaf rubber stamp* and ink pads

For Contemporary Album Cover
* 1 unpainted wooden album cover (10" x 12" (25.5 x 30.5))*
* Unpainted wooden trims: 1 long scroll (10.625" x 2.5" (27 x 6.5 cm)), 1 round face (5.75" x 6" (14.5 x 15 cm)), 2 squares (2" x 2" (5 x 5 cm))*
* Metallic copper gilt
* Paints: weathered copper textured spray, copper green acrylic craft
* Wood glue
* Miscellaneous items: 1" (2.5 cm) sponge brush, paint palette, fine sandpaper, tack cloth, ruler, pencil, sheet of paper, scissors, saw

*(See Sources on pg. 159 for purchasing information.)

Lightly sand all outer surfaces of box and album covers; remove dust with tack cloth. Refer to page 156 for Painting Instructions and Techniques. Use sponge brush to basecoat all outer surfaces of document box and lid with turquoise and outer side of both 6" x 9" (15 x 23 cm) album covers with metallic gold.

DOCUMENT BOX

See illustration to apply paints to rubber stamps in desired colors, and stamp randomly on box top. Practice stamping on scrap paper first. Press the rubber stamp firmly and evenly. Do not roll; apply more paint to the stamp as necessary. Follow manufacturer's instructions to emboss patterns on box top. Apply embossing liquid randomly; sprinkle embossing powders on, mixing the colors together. Apply heat source to the powders until liquid disappears.

DECOUPAGED ALBUM COVER

1 *Apply crackle medium* with sponge brush over gold paint, following manufacturer's instructions. Use sponge brush to paint off-white over the crackle medium.

2 *Stamp leaves in desired colors* onto paper. Arrange leaves on front cover; apply leaves with decoupage medium, following manufacturer's instructions. Seal entire cover with decoupage medium as shown in illustration.

CONTEMPORARY ALBUM COVER

1 *Remove hinges and posts* from album covers and spray outer side of both covers with copper textured paint, following manufacturer's instructions. Let dry.

2 *Place long scroll* on hinge side of album cover. Refer to photo and illustration to mark a line lengthwise with pencil and ruler on long scroll so it will fit along album edge. Carefully cut the long scroll with saw. Basecoat the long scroll pieces, round face and 2 squares with copper green craft paint and sponge brush.

3 *Dry-brush or buff copper gilt* on the high spots of the trims, front and back album cover edges, album hinges and post heads. Glue the trims onto album cover as shown in the photo, and install hinges and posts.

Pine Needle
Basket

***B**ring the wonderful scent* of pine into your home with this 6" (15 cm) round basket. Collect your own pine needles or purchase them ready to coil a durable basket. Shaping the basket is accomplished by sewing one coil on top of another, and the pattern comes from the pine needle sheath ends.

LIST of MATERIALS

❋ Dried pine needles, at least 4" (10 cm) long (See Sources on pg. 159 for purchasing information.)
❋ Waxed linen thread
❋ Large tapestry needle
❋ Miscellaneous items: scissors, newspapers, bucket, tape measure

1 *Preparation:* Purchase pine needles, or gather clean, flexible needles. Spread needles on newspapers and let dry in a dark, well-ventilated area. Do not use undried needles, as basket will shrink and loosen as it dries.

2 *Base Center:* Soak needles overnight and keep moist while coiling. Thread tapestry needle with linen thread. Align 3 or 4 thin, or 1 or 2 thick, pine needles, sheath ends together. Form sheath end of needles into a small loop, as in the Step 2 illustration.

3 *Coiling Base:* See the Step 3A illustration to stitch first coil, by bending wrapped needles to form a circle. See 3B to begin second coil. Insert additional pine needles as needed, keeping coil a consistent thickness. Add thread when needed by knotting thread ends. Continue coiling until base diameter measures approximately 2½" (6.5 cm).

4 *Basket Sides:* Shape and enlarge the basket by sewing the next coil slightly overlapping previous coil and angling outward. Sew 2 or 3 rows in this manner.

5 *Sheath Pattern:* Align a bundle of 4 or 5 needles, sheaths together, on top of previous coil. See the Step 5 illustration. Begin a new bundle of needles every fifth or seventh stitch in a spiraling pattern. Continue 10 or 12 rows in this manner or until diameter measures approximately 6" (15 cm).

6 *Basket Top:* Angle rows inward rather than outward on the upper half of basket, inserting needles into coil rather than placing them on top. Vary the pattern with 1 sheathed needle per stitch. Coil in this manner for 5 or 6 rows. To finish coiling, reduce number of needles and coil until you have a 2½" (6.5 cm) opening.

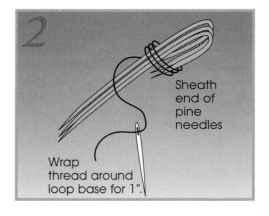

2

Sheath end of pine needles

Wrap thread around loop base for 1".

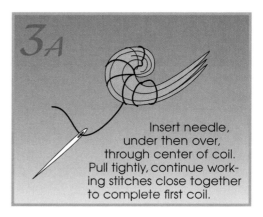

3A

Insert needle, under then over, through center of coil. Pull tightly, continue working stitches close together to complete first coil.

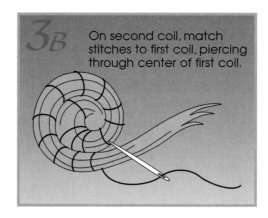

3B

On second coil, match stitches to first coil, piercing through center of first coil.

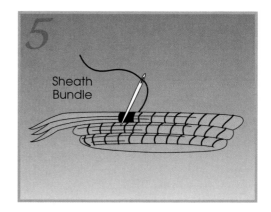

5

Sheath Bundle

Visitors will be delighted with a uniquely decorated towel in the guest bathroom. Yo yos tacked on a bath towel make the pretty basket that doubles as a pocket for holding a facecloth. Yellow and blue make a dynamic impact on this towel, or use colors to complement your decor.

* Bath towel and facecloth
* 51 purchased yo yos or 45" (115 cm) cotton fabrics, 1/8 yd. (0.15 m) each of 8 yellow, blue and white coordinating prints
* 1" (2.5 cm) gold grosgrain ribbon, 3/4 yd. (0.7 m)
* Sewing threads to match fabrics
* Miscellaneous items: scissors, sewing needle, compass, straight pins

TIPS and IDEAS

* Purchase premade yo yos and these towels will do up in a snap.
* For a shower gift, fill the basket with packets of bubble bath, bottles of scented lotions or decorative soaps.
* Use whatever color scheme will accent your decor, the season or the holiday.

1 Wash and dry towel, facecloth and purchased yo yos or yo yo fabrics to remove sizing.

2 If you are making your own yo yos, cut fifty-one 2³/4" (7 cm) circles from assorted fabrics. See page 158 for instructions on how to make yo yos.

3 Refer to the illustration to arrange yo yos in basket shape. Tack yo yos together, beginning at the basket base and moving up to the basket handle. Tack handle yo yos together in a long strand.

4 Center basket and pin on towel 6" (15 cm) from bottom edge. Hand-sew sides and bottom of basket base to towel. Sew handle to towel.

5 Tie ribbon bow and tack to 1 side of basket handle. Fold and insert facecloth into basket.

Autumn ANGELS

Charming angels dressed

In vibrant fall colors drift across the
heavens on leaf wings inspired by the
spirit of autumn. Copper foil is baked in
the oven to transform them into colorful
heavenly wings, and bits of dried flowers,
leaves and berries complement their
natural looks.

LIST of MATERIALS

For each angel – approximately 13" (33 cm) tall

❋ 4¹/₂" (11.5 cm) wood doll cutout or use pattern and cut your own

❋ Acrylic paints: apricot, rose, black, orange, green, yellow

❋ Paintbrushes: No. 10 flat, small round fabric

❋ Spanish moss

❋ ¹/₄" (6 mm) sticks, two each: 3¹/₂" (9 cm) for arms; 6¹/₂" (16.3 cm) for legs

❋ 45" (115 cm) cotton fabrics: ¹/₄ yd. (0.25 m) orange, green or yellow for dress; ¹/₄ yd. (0.25 m) peach, natural or light yellow for apron

❋ Copper tooling foil, 6" (15 cm) square, two

❋ Punching awl

❋ 18-gauge copper wire, 20" (51 cm)

❋ Assorted trims: 2" (5 cm) sinamay hat (orange angel); ¹/₈" (3 mm) satin ribbon, your choice, ²/₃ yd. (0.63 m) (orange and yellow angels); small dried florals/naturals

❋ Low-temp glue gun

❋ Pattern Sheet

❋ Miscellaneous items: disposable palette, wire cutters, scissors, ruler, fine-point black permanent marker, sewing needle, matching threads, iron, tracing paper, pencil, masking tape, empty ballpoint pen, newspapers, fine steel wool, cookie sheet, oven, sewing machine, sandpaper

TIPS and IDEAS

❋ Personalize your angel by writing a name, verse or quotation across her bottom apron edge.

1 Painting: Refer to page 156 for Painting Instructions and Techniques. Paint wood doll face apricot. Use fabric brush to stipple cheeks with rose. Dot black for eyes. Paint remainder of doll orange, green or yellow; let dry. Glue Spanish moss hair to head.

2 *Cutting:* Cut one 6¼" x 20" (15.7 x 51 cm) skirt, two 2¼" x 4" (6 x 10 cm) sleeves, and two ½" x 2½" (1.3 x 6.5 cm) leg tabs from dress fabric. Cut one 5½" x 20" (14 x 51 cm) apron from apron fabric.

3 *Legs:* Fold a leg tab in half widthwise. Glue ¾" (2 cm) of each tab end to top of leg stick. To attach leg to doll, glue extending fabric to center bottom, as shown in the illustration.

4 *Skirt & Apron:* Press fabrics. Pull threads to fringe 1 long skirt and apron edge. Use black marker to write message along bottom apron edge. Place apron on skirt, right sides up, matching top edges. Sew gathering stitch along top edge through both layers of fabric. Pull thread to gather, and refer to photo to glue around doll waist.

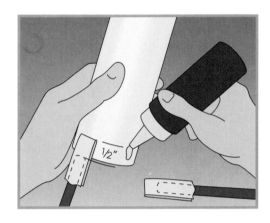

5 *Arms:* Fold sleeves lengthwise in half and press flat. Trim raw edges straight. See the Step 5 illustration and, for outstretched arms, wrap and spot-glue sleeve around stick arm, matching raw edge of sleeve with stick end. For bent arms, repeat with raw sleeve edge extending ¼" (6 mm) above top of stick. Refer to photo to glue arms to doll.

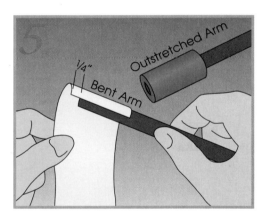

6 *Wing Pattern:* Choose desired leaf pattern and trace 2, reversing 1, onto tracing paper. Tape patterns to copper foil square. Use empty ballpoint pen to trace onto foil. Apply just enough pressure to indent foil. Remove pattern. Place foil on newspapers and use awl to punch holes along vein lines approximately ⅛" (3 mm) apart.

7 *Wings:* Cut out leaf wings. Turn to wrong side and use empty ballpoint pen to draw an outline ¹⁄₁₆" (1.5 mm) from edge. Rub front of leaf with steel wool to remove fingerprints. Preheat oven to 325°F (160°C). Place leaves on cookie sheet and bake for 15 to 20 minutes. Remove leaves when copper turns colors; cool. Glue leaf wings to center back of doll.

8 *Hanger:* Bend wire into a circle, twisting ends together. Glue twisted wire joint to angel back between wings. Spot-glue wire along back of wings. Add bits of dried florals/naturals to hide glue. Refer to photo to glue dried florals/naturals to angel hands. Tie ribbon bows and glue to hat and bouquet.

Ribbon
EMBROIDERY LAMP SHADE

*G*ive *a plain* Jane lamp shade, or a weary old one, a beauty makeover with a bouquet of ribbon flowers. Embroider the petaled posies on damask fabric, and in no time you're ready to cover the lamp shade frame. A soft lamplight glow lets you indulge in the splendor of these flowers throughout the evening hours.

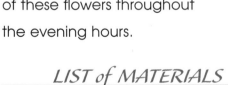

LIST *of* MATERIALS

* ❋ 4" (10 cm) plain clip-on lamp shade
* ❋ Ecru damask fabric, 9" x 11" (23 x 28 cm)
* ❋ Bucilla 100% silk ribbon in colors listed on Color Key
* ❋ Baby green (966) pearl cotton
* ❋ White embroidery floss
* ❋ Needles: Six No. 24 tapestry, embroidery
* ❋ ½" (1.3 cm) ecru gimp braid, ½ yd. (0.5 m)
* ❋ Black permanent marker
* ❋ Liquid fray preventer
* ❋ Glues: white craft, hot glue gun
* ❋ Pattern Sheet
* ❋ Miscellaneous items: pencil, tracing paper, vanishing-ink pen, sharp scissors, tape measure, masking tape, iron

1 *Lamp Shade Pattern:* Wrap tracing paper around shade; trace the top and bottom edges with pencil. Use the vanishing-ink pen to trace pattern on right side of damask fabric, adding ½" (1.3 cm) to one short end. Do not cut out.

2 *Embroidery Design:* Use the black marker to trace design to tracing paper. Center tracing behind damask with design ¾" (2 cm) above shade bottom. Transfer the design with the vanishing-ink pen.

3 *Embroidery:* Refer to page 155 for Ribbon Embroidery Instructions and Stitches. Use a different needle for each ribbon color and width to minimize waste. Thread each needle with a 12" (30.5 cm) length of ribbon or 1 strand of pearl cotton. Lock each ribbon on the needle. To end, tie a slip knot on wrong side.

4 *Stitches:* Work stitches in the order given in the Color Key beginning with 4- and 5-loop flowers with ½" (1.3 cm) petals. Work a French knot with 2 wraps at the center of each loop flower using sunflower ribbon. Work all other French knots with 1 wrap, filling in with additional knots as desired.

5 *Covering the Lamp Shade:* Press damask around embroidered design; cut out along pattern lines and apply liquid fray preventer to seal edges. Beginning at shade seam, squeeze 3 evenly spaced dots of hot glue on shade top edge. Align damask upper corner with first glue dot and adhere fabric to shade. Use dots of glue to prevent glue from seeping. Repeat to glue damask to bottom edge, smoothing fabric around shade. Turn 1 short fabric end under ¼" (6 mm); overlap and glue seam.

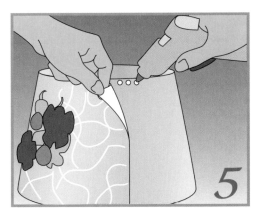

6 *Finishing:* Measure and cut 2 lengths of braid 1" (2.5 cm) longer than top and bottom circumference of shade. Wrap tape around ½" (1.3 cm) of each braid end. Starting at seam and leaving taped end unglued, glue braid around shade top covering raw fabric edge. Butt braid, then cut off taped ends. Coat ends with craft glue to prevent fraying. Repeat for bottom of shade.

Mosaic Bottle
& PICTURE FRAME

Mosaic has been in use as art since the
third century B.C., so it's about time you tried it. Mosaics
can be applied to just about any surface that won't give
(or the tile design will break apart). The design can be
abstract and helter-skelter, or precision planned
and detailed. Either way, mosaic is easy—just
follow the steps below.

LIST of MATERIALS

For Both Projects
* Tile adhesive*
* Tile grout*
* Craft sticks
* Mosaic tile nipper*
* Safety glasses
* Latex or vinyl disposable gloves

For Fish Bottle
* Glass long-neck bottle
* 1" (2.5 cm) mosaic tiles*: black,
  white, green, tan, brown and
  various shades of blue
* Pattern Sheet

For Picture Frame
* Picture frame
* 1" (2.5 cm) mosaic tiles*: red,
  yellow, blue, black
* Miscellaneous items: tracing
  paper, graphite paper, marker,
  pencil, tape, sponge, paper towels
*(See Sources on pg. 159 for
  purchasing information.)

FISH BOTTLE

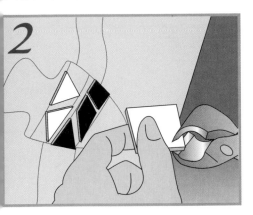

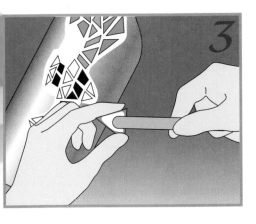

1 *Preparation:* Wash bottle with warm water, and remove any labels and label residue. Let dry. Trace pattern onto tracing paper. Either draw rough outlines freehand with marker onto bottle, or trace pattern main outlines with graphite paper.

2 *Tiles:* Place pattern on flat surface. Wear safety glasses and begin to nip tiles to fit pattern in appropriate colors. Lay on the pattern as shown in Step 2 illustration. If you do not have nippers, you can put tiles in a freezer-weight plastic bag and smash them with a hammer. Any kind of material—rocks, plates, terra-cotta pots, china, marbles, etc.—will work well for mosaic materials. Ideally, all materials should be the same depth, or an uneven surface will appear.

3 *Gluing:* Put on disposable gloves and lay the bottle on its side. Begin by squeezing a bead of adhesive onto the bottle, and spread it around with the trowel tool, making ridges. Work with a small area at a time for best results. Use craft stick to spread tile adhesive on the back, textured side of tile; see Step 3 illustration. Begin with the fish design first, then the seaweed, shell and starfish. Complete the rest of the bottle with various shades of blue, letting the adhesive set about 30 minutes before turning the bottle. Place tiles onto the project with the smooth side up and textured side down. Try to leave 1/8" (3 mm) or less between the tile pieces. Let adhesive set the recommended time before going on to the next step.

4 *Grouting:* Spread grout onto the tiles with a craft stick or putty knife. Work the grout into the spaces between the tiles until the grout is smooth and level with the tile surface. Wipe off excess grout with a damp sponge. When the grout has thoroughly dried, polish the tile surface with a damp paper towel until the tiles are shiny and free of any grout residue.

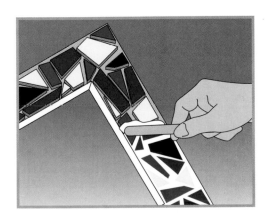

PICTURE FRAME

Repeat Steps 2-4 above to finish picture frame, gluing blue, black, yellow and red tile pieces randomly onto the frame.

Dino-Mite
DINOSAUR

Kids love dinosaurs, and this fancy purplesaurus with protruding, purple peepers and a fluffy feather-trimmed rose bow is no exception. The secret of her luxurious, velvety texture is rich purple velour fabric.

LIST of MATERIALS

- ⅓ yd. (0.32 m) purple velour
- 9" x 12" (23 x 30.5 cm) white felt
- 2 oz. (50 g) polyester fiberfill
- 5 mm lavender pom-poms, two
- ¼" (6 mm) purple satin ribbon, ⅓ yd. (0.32 m)
- 2 purple large rocaille beads
- Glitter fabric paints: purple, crystal

- Magenta pink cloth rosebud with leaves
- Lavender marabou feather
- Sewing threads: purple, magenta pink
- Stuffing tool or forceps
- Hot glue gun
- Pattern Sheet
- Miscellaneous items: sewing machine, needle, pins, scissors, tracing paper, pencil, wire cutters

1 *Preparation:* Cut felt into two 6" x 9" (15 X 23 cm) pieces. Cut the velour into one 12" (30.5 cm) square and two 6" x 9" (15 X 23 cm) pieces lengthwise with the fabric grain.

2 *Pattern:* Transfer dorsal spike pattern to the center of each felt piece, reversing 1. **Do not cut out.** Trace remaining patterns and cut from 12" (30.5 cm) square of velour folded right sides together.

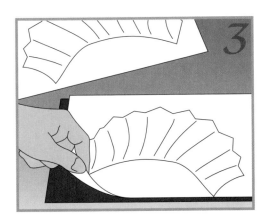

3 *Dorsal Spike:* Place each 6" x 9" (15 x 23 cm) felt piece, tracing side up, on wrong side of a 6" x 9" (15 x 23 cm) velour piece. Use magenta pink thread to topstitch on quilting lines. Cut out on bold cutting outlines. Place spike pieces purple sides together and use purple thread to sew 1/4" (6 mm) seams. Clip curves and turn. Use stuffing tool or forceps to gently push out all edges and points.

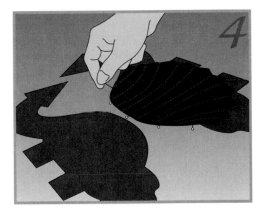

4 *Assembly:* Use purple thread and sew pieces right sides together in 1/4" (6 mm) seams. See Step 4 illustration to sandwich the spike upside down between the body pieces and sew seams over back between Points A and B. Sew gusset to body leaving open between Points C. Sew remaining seams. Clip curves and turn. Solidly pack fiberfill in the tail, legs and head. Slipstitch opening closed.

5 *Eyes:* Insert needle through both eyes pulling thread tightly several times; knot thread. Glue pom-pom eyes into sockets. Dot each eye with purple glitter paint.

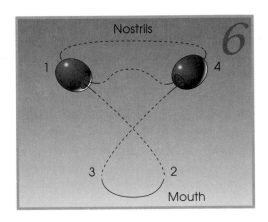

6 *Nostrils & Mouth:* See the Step 6 illustration to anchor thread at 1, string bead, stitch in at 1, out at 4, string bead, and stitch in at 4. Stitch back and forth several times between 1 and 4; knot thread. For mouth, insert needle at 1, stitch through bead, stitch out at 2, in at 3, out at 4 and go through bead. Repeat, pulling thread tight; knot thread. Trace over mouth threads with crystal glitter paint.

7 *Finishing:* Tie ribbon around neck with bow at top of head. Clip stem off rosebud. Trim feather to 3" (7.5 cm) and glue to underside of rose. Glue rose with feather to center top of bow.

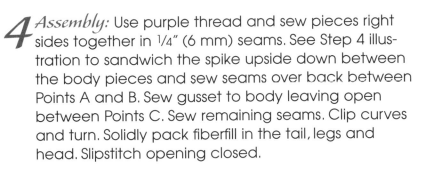

No card can express your innermost feelings better than you. And what better way to background your written thoughts than with stationery that you make yourself. Inexpensive paper and envelopes are dressed in napkins blotted with food coloring to produce marbleized textured writing papers on which to say, "I love you!"

LIST of MATERIALS

* White or pastel paper, postcards and envelopes
* Liquid food coloring: red, yellow, blue, green
* Inexpensive white or pastel single-ply paper napkins
* Spray adhesive
* Miscellaneous items: scissors, craft knife, metal ruler, 4 small containers for food coloring, iron, cookie sheet, metal tablespoon, flat paintbrush or 2" (5 cm) square sponge

1 *Preparation:* In each container, dilute 3 drops of each food coloring in ¼ cup (50 mL) water. Unfold and place napkin flat on work surface.

2 *Marbling:* Apply food colorings to napkin using 1 of these methods: drizzle coloring from spoon, splatter coloring from paintbrush bristles, or sponge coloring onto napkin. See the Step 2 illustration for how to sponge. Leave some areas of napkin uncolored.

3 *Drying:* Place napkin on cookie sheet in a 170° to 200°F (76° to 95°C) oven with door open, watching carefully until dry (30 to 60 seconds). Press napkin with iron on low heat setting.

4 *Writing Paper:* Follow spray adhesive manufacturer's instructions to spray back of a sheet of paper with adhesive. Place paper, adhesive side down, over napkin as shown in the illustration. Position close to edge to have enough leftover napkin to cover matching envelope flap. Press paper with iron to adhere napkin. Use ruler to trim napkin along paper edges using craft knife.

5 *Envelope:* Open flap and place envelope, adhesive side down, on work surface. Spray adhesive on excess napkin. Place napkin, adhesive side down, over flap and align napkin edge with flap crease. Press with iron to adhere napkin. Use ruler to trim napkin along envelope flap edges using craft knife; see the Step 5 illustration.

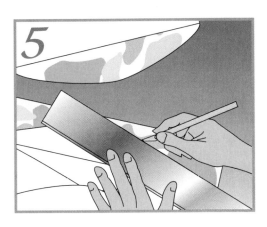

6 *Postcard:* Repeat Steps 2-4.

Mini Adirondack
CHAIR

The appeal of miniature furniture has expanded far beyond the traditional dollhouse. In today's matchless mix of home furnishings, it's not uncommon to find one's favorite period piece, à la petite, tucked into a bookcase or displayed on a mantel, end table or dresser top. This 6" (15 cm) high Adirondack chair (also known as a Kennebunkport chair) with its deep seat and angled back, is the original lawn chair, simply made from jumbo craft sticks painted bright white.

LIST of MATERIALS

* Jumbo craft sticks
* White acrylic craft paint
* No. 10 flat paintbrush
* Clear acrylic sealer
* Scroll saw

* White craft glue
* Pattern Sheet
* Miscellaneous items: tracing paper, pencil, stylus, ruler, fine sandpaper, scissors, 5 spring clothespins, 2 heavy books

1 *Preparation:* Select only flat craft sticks, as even slightly warped ones will distort the design. Trace the patterns onto tracing paper and cut out. Sand edges smooth.

2 *Chair Back:* Refer to the Step 2 illustration to position 3 braces horizontally on a flat surface. Position 5 sticks as back slats, vertically, on top. Glue in place; let dry. Trace the chair back pattern on glued slats and cut with scroll saw. Sand edges. **Do not cut off** 1/2" (1.3 cm) extensions of middle brace.

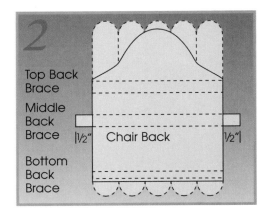

3 *Chair Seat:* Run a line of glue on top edge of each seat side. On flat surface, position sides 4" (10 cm) apart, parallel, and upright (glued edge up). Prop up with books. Starting 1/4" (6 mm) from front and back, place seat slats across sides, evenly spaced and with ends aligned with side edges. Let dry. Glue seat front to side front edges.

4 *Attaching Chair Back to Chair Seat:* Refer to the Step 4 illustration and trace the back/seat angle onto tracing paper. Extend lines using ruler. Place tracing on flat surface. Run a glue line along the edge of the back seat slat. Place seat and back on their sides, positioning on top of traced angle, and glue together. To hold in place, support back and seat with a book; let dry.

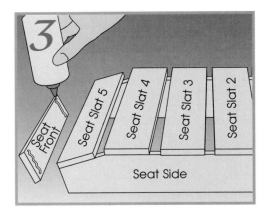

5 *Legs & Arms:* Refer to the photo and glue front legs to sides flush with seat front and extending 1 3/16" (3 cm) above seat. Glue back legs at an angle. Place chair on flat surface and adjust legs so that chair is level. If necessary, hold legs to sides with clothespins while drying. Center and glue arms on top of center back brace extensions and front legs.

6 *Finishing:* Paint chair with 2 or more coats of paint. Let dry. Apply several coats of acrylic sealer, following manufacturer's instructions.

Rose Topiary Centerpiece
& PLACECARD HOLDERS

Do something out of the ordinary with those roses! Instead of putting them in a vase, which blocks everyone's view at the table, create a more slender centerpiece by twining them into a topiary. For a formal setting, make placecard holders from individual rosebuds. All are planted in terra-cotta pots that you gild yourself.

LIST of MATERIALS

For Both Projects
* Floral foam for live arrangements
* Gold foil and foil adhesive
* 1" (2.5 cm) sponge brush
* Acrylic high-gloss sealer
* Moss and greening pins
* Sharp kitchen knife or floral cutters
* Miscellaneous items: sandpaper, scissors, serrated knife, leather gloves, ruler, masking tape

For Topiary
* 6" (15 cm) terra-cotta pot, pot liner
* 12-18 live long-stemmed roses
* 3 yd. (2.75 m) gold ribbon, 1" (2.5 cm) wide

For Each Placecard Holder
* 3" (7.5 cm) terra-cotta pot, pot liner
* 1 rose
* ½ yd. (0.5 m) gold ribbon, 1" (2.5 cm) wide

TIPS and IDEAS

* Substitute dried roses for fresh, for a longer-lasting arrangement.
* Gilded terra-cotta pots look elegant; paint or decoupage instead for a more casual feel.
* Does gilding sound like it takes too long? Simply use metallic gold spray paint on the planter pots.

TOPIARY

1 **Preparation:** Lightly sand any rough spots on terra-cotta pot. Wash with warm water only; let dry. Do not use any detergent or glass cleaners. Holding rose stems with leather gloves, remove all leaves and thorns from rose stems. Cut ribbon into three 1-yd. (0.95 m) pieces.

JAMES ELLSWORTH

2 Gold Foiling: Follow manufacturer's instructions to apply foil adhesive randomly to outer surface of pot. When adhesive is dry, but still tacky, apply gold foil following manufacturer's instructions. Refer to the Step 2 illustration, working in small areas at a time. Use sponge brush to help in foil application. Apply gold foil along the rim and saucer as well.

3 Topiary Base: Let foil dry thoroughly; apply 2 coats of sealer to the pot inside and out following manufacturer's instructions. Cut floral foam to fit firmly into pot liner with serrated knife. Remove foam, and soak thoroughly in water with any desired floral preservatives. Place foam in liner, and liner in pot.

4 Making the Topiary: Grasp roses 6" (15 cm) below the flowers. Arrange the blooms so they create a nice rounded mound suitable for a topiary. Refer to the photo and the illustration to wrap the bundle of stems with a piece of masking tape about 2" (5 cm) below flowers. Wrap tightly enough to hold the roses, but not so you damage the stems.

5 Placement: Hold topiary next to pot, as shown in illustration, and decide how tall you want your centerpiece; leave long enough stems to hold them in the pot. If necessary, cut the rose stems to the desired height with sharp knife or floral cutters in a sink of warm water. Grasp the topiary firmly in 1 hand and with the other work the stems into the floral foam.

6 Finishing: Take 1 ribbon piece and center it around the topiary stem, covering masking tape. Refer to the photo to tie the ribbon, and then crisscross it down the stem. Cover the top of the floral foam with moss, and hold moss and ribbon ends in place with greening pins. Tie remaining ribbon pieces on as streamers.

PLACECARD HOLDERS

Refer to Steps 1-3 above, except leave uppermost leaves in place on roses. Cut stem, and place a single rosebud in terra-cotta pot. Make a bow from ribbon. Secure it and moss with a greening pin.

Don't hide those favorite pictures of your sand-between-the-toes gang! Sparkling beaches and sparkling smiles are preserved using a decoupage technique on a clear plate. Follow these easy instructions to get the nitty-gritty on making this fun and easy remembrance!

LIST of MATERIALS

* Photos, approximately 6
* 13" (33 cm) clear glass plate with a flat bottom
* Acrylic paints: turquoise, cappuccino, white
* Paintbrushes: ½" (1.3 cm) stencil, ¾" (2 cm) flat
* Ultra fine-point gold marker
* Assorted small seashells
* Glues: decoupage, white craft
* Pattern Sheet
* Miscellaneous items: piece of paper, tracing paper, pencil, scissors, single-edge razor blade, paper towels

1 *Preparation:* Place plate facedown on work surface. Place the sheet of paper on top of the plate. Press the paper down and trace the circle outline of the plate base, not plate outer edge, with a pencil. See Step 1 illustration to arrange the photos on the paper and trim them to fit within the traced circle; photos may overlap.

2 *Decoupaging:* Apply a thin coat of decoupage glue to the front of the photos with a flat brush and press them to the back of the plate. Check placement from front of plate. Press the back of the photos to remove any air bubbles. Let dry until they are no longer tacky. Decoupage glue will dry completely clear in 2 to 3 days.

3 *Ocean Spray:* Refer to the photo for placement of the different paint colors; let dry between coats. Dip stencil brush in white paint; blot excess onto a paper towel. Hold the brush to the side and gently dab the paint on the front of the plate, creating a thin edge. See the Step 3 illustration to raise the brush to a straight up-and-down position so that the color will be almost solid in the middle but frothy around the edges. Work until the entire spray line is complete.

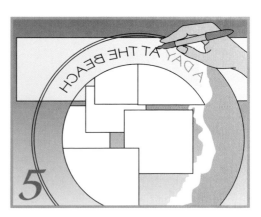

4 *Sand:* Use the flat brush to paint cappuccino onto the back of the plate up to and below the ocean spray.

5 *Lettering:* Trace the lettering pattern. Refer to the photo for placement and tape pattern on the plate front along the rim. Turn plate over and trace letters (they will be reversed) onto the back side of the plate with the gold marker, as shown in the Step 5 illustration. To remove a mistake, use razor blade and begin again.

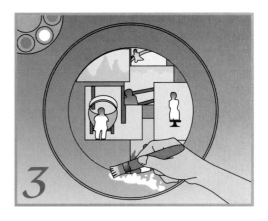

6 *Water:* With the plate facedown, cover the lettering and water area with turquoise paint and flat brush. Apply a second coat of both cappuccino and turquoise.

7 *Finishing:* Apply 2-3 coats of decoupage glue over the entire back of the plate. When the plate is completely dry, glue an interesting arrangement of shells to the front of the plate in the sand area.

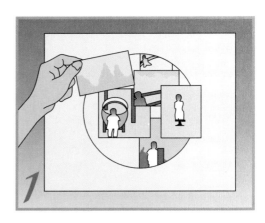

Rubber Stamp
NOTECARDS

Personalize that letter or thank-you note with cards that you make yourself. You don't have to be an artist—rubber stamps and water-color markers make it easy. The recipient will treasure the notecards themselves as much as the message.

LIST of MATERIALS

For Each Notecard
* 8½" x 11" (21.8 x 28 cm) ivory parchment card stock
* Olive green pigment stamp pad*
* No. 4 shader paintbrush
* Paint palette

For Girl Notecards
* Rubber stamps*: girl with braids, flower button, heart button, star button, small sunflower
* Watercolor brush markers*: green, pink, purple, red, yellow, orange, brown

For Sunflower Notecards
* Rubber stamps*: large sunflower, apple, pear
* Watercolor brush markers*: red, green, orange, yellow, brown
* White acrylic craft paint

Miscellaneous items: ruler, pencil, water container

*(See Sources on pg. 159 for purchasing information.)

EACH NOTECARD

1 Card: Fold cardstock in half twice to make a card 4¼" x 5½" (10.8 x 14 cm). See the illustration to divide the card front into blocks by lightly tracing around the stamp backs.

2 *Stamping:* Press the rubber stamp firmly and evenly onto the stamp pad, then onto the paper inside the blocks. Do not roll the stamp when pressing it on the pad or paper. Re-ink the stamp after each use. Refer to photo for placement.

3 *Coloring:* Use the watercolor brush markers. Tap the marker on the palette to release a small puddle of paint to blend and shade the colors. Thin with a small amount of water, if desired. Then dip the paintbrush into the mixture and apply as indicated. Refer to photo for colors.

GIRL NOTECARDS

1 *Trace over the pencil lines* with green marker. Stamp the designs within the appropriate blocks as shown in the Step 1 illustration and photo. Using the pink marker, fill in the blank blocks with random dots.

2 *Refer to Coloring* to paint the girl's dress and hat green; combine brown and yellow to paint the hair and shoes. Color in the flowers, apron and hat ornaments with pink and purple markers.

3 *Refer to Coloring* to paint sunflower centers with yellow, orange and red. Refer to the photo to color in the remaining stamp designs and backgrounds with the markers. Paint the outer border with thinned green.

SUNFLOWER NOTECARDS

1 *Trace over the pencil lines* with red marker. Stamp the designs within the appropriate blocks. See Coloring to paint: sunflower leaves yellow, green and red; stems green and brown; petals yellow, orange and brown; and flower centers yellow, orange, red and brown.

2 *Using the red marker,* fill in the blank blocks on the border with random dots and vertical and horizontal stripes as shown in the illustration. See Coloring to paint the pears and apples red, yellow and orange and the leaves green and brown. Use paintbrush to highlight fruit and sunflower randomly with white acrylic paint.

*M*arbleized
PEDESTALS

*S*imple sponging techniques and gold foil accents transform plaster into exquisite faux marble pedestals that are easy on your pocketbook and will look elegant in your home! Lovely plant stands for a foyer, they're also a gorgeous way to display some of those treasures hidden away in cupboards or closets.

LIST of MATERIALS

For Each Project
* Plaster pedestal
* Exterior gloss varnish
* Foil adhesive
* Foil sheets: gold, silver (black marble only)
* Paintbrushes: liner, flat, sponge

For Rose Marble
* Acrylic paints: ivory, antique rose, Cape Cod blue, apple green, straw, gold gleam

For Black Marble
* Waterbase spray-on color: black, ivory, apricot, gold glitter
* Acrylic paints: light ivory, pink angel
* Miscellaneous items: sandpaper, tack cloth, disposable palette, natural sea sponge, water spray bottle, feather (optional)

TIPS and IDEAS

* Use a different paint color for the basecoat to match your decor.
* Find a marbleized finish you like in a spray can, apply it and go right to Step 3 to complete with gold foil.

Lightly sand rough areas on each pedestal and wipe with tack cloth. Refer to page 156 for Painting Instructions and Techniques. Apply a coat of varnish and let dry.

ROSE MARBLE

1 *Basecoat with 2 coats* of ivory; let dry. Paint any motifs such as the flower antique rose and leaves apple green. Paint 1 top band blue and remaining bands straw. On remaining pedestal areas, use a damp sponge to randomly sponge antique rose; see illustration. Sponge antique rose/ivory mix; let dry.

2 *Brush foil adhesive* onto top straw-painted bands and corner pedestal curves. Apply adhesive heavily for a solid gold leaf look, or lightly for light gold accents. Let adhesive dry until clear. Refer to manufacturer's instructions to apply foil.

3 *Use a liner brush or feather* to randomly paint gold vein lines on pedestal to simulate marble. Dab lines with a damp sponge to soften. Let dry for 24 hours. Apply 2 coats of varnish.

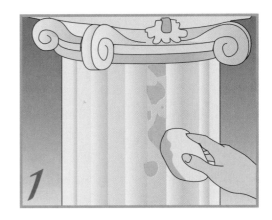

BLACK MARBLE

1 *Spray pedestal* with black waterbase color; while still wet, mist with water to soften black. While black is still wet, randomly spray apricot, then ivory. Let some color run for a natural look. Soften some areas with a damp sponge as desired.

2 *Thin light ivory and pink angel* with water. Randomly sponge colors on pedestal for desired look; let dry. Lightly spray entire pedestal with gold glitter; let dry.

3 *Brush adhesive* onto top and bottom pedestal bands. To create slightly raised gold areas, use the sea sponge to randomly sponge adhesive onto pedestal. Thin adhesive with water to the consistency of cream. Use liner brush or feather to apply random vein lines to simulate marble. Let adhesive dry until clear.

4 *Refer to the manufacturer's instructions* to apply gold foil to vein lines. Alternately apply gold and silver foil onto remaining adhesive-covered areas. Let dry for 24 hours. Apply 2 coats of varnish.

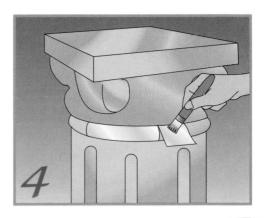

Victorian BARRETTES

Stitch a delicate floral design on black evenweave fabric for a dressy Victorian look. Choose from a bouquet of pink flowers or a spray of pansies. Attach to a premade padded barrette, called a pillow clip, and you have an accessory that's sure to add a special touch to your wardrobe.

LIST of MATERIALS

For Each Barrette

* 18-count black Aida cloth, 6" x 12" (15 x 30.5 cm)
* Oval pillow clip (See Sources on pg. 159 for purchasing information.)
* Hot glue gun
* No. 24 tapestry needle
* DMC 6-strand embroidery floss listed on Color Key, 1 skein each

1 *Refer to page 155* for Cross-Stitch Instructions and Stitches. Cross-stitch each design using 2 strands of floss.

2 *Work backstitches* on the pansy design using 1 strand of black. Follow manufacturer's instructions to attach stitched design to pillow clip.

PANSIES

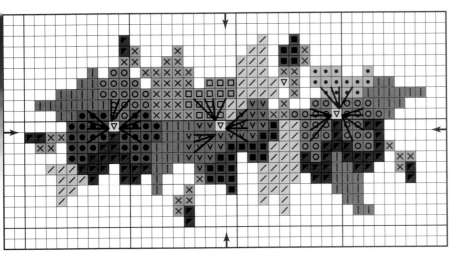

PANSIES COLOR KEY

Symbol	Name	DMC
◪	Dark Violet	208
●	Medium Violet	209
○	Violet	210
·	Light Liolet	211
■	Dark Purple	550
∨	Medium Purple	553
□	Purple	554
I	Dark Olive	730
✕	Olive	732
╱	Light Olive	733
▽	Ecru	-----
—	Black Backstitches	310

PINK FLOWERS

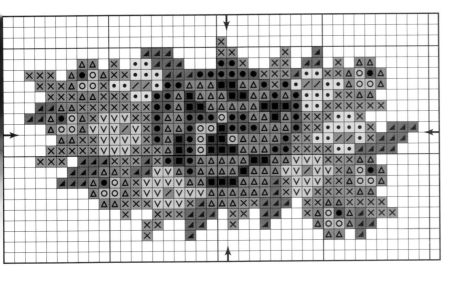

PINK FLOWERS COLOR KEY

Symbol	Name	DMC
■	Dark Pink	3685
●	Medium Pink	3687
△	Pink	3688
○	Light Pink	3689
╱	Gold	680
∨	Gray Green	928
◣	Dark Green	520
✕	Green	522
·	Ecru	-----

Sunflower
SLIP-ONS

These slip-ons aren't sold in stores, but you can make them yourself. A catchy sunflower painted on the folded tongue completely revamps an ordinary canvas shoe into a trendsetting change from summer sandals or sneakers. Once your friends see these snappy shoes, they'll want a pair, too!

LIST of MATERIALS

* White canvas sneakers
* Yellow spray paint
* Acrylic paints: burnt umber, burnt sienna, antique gold, black, medium green, dark pine, cream
* Paintbrushes: Nos. 6 and 8 flat, No. 1 liner
* Clear silicone glue
* Miscellaneous items: white transfer paper, heavy-duty scissors, pencil, tracing paper, masking tape, disposable palette, paper towels, water container

1 *Refer to the photo and Step 1 illustration* to cut out the side/eyelet panels on each shoe. Spray paint inside and outside of shoes with 2-3 light coats of yellow; let dry thoroughly between coats. Fold tongue of each shoe over the toe and temporarily tape to shoe.

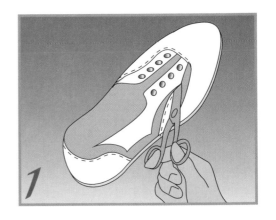

2 *Trace the pattern* onto tracing paper. Transfer sunflower to tongue. Remove tape and transfer leaves to each side of shoe front.

3 *Refer to page 156* for Painting Instructions and Techniques. Use flat brush to basecoat the leaves with medium green. Sideload brush with dark pine and shade 1 side of each leaf as shown in photo.

4 *Highlight each leaf center* with touch of antique gold. Using liner brush and dark pine, refer to the photo to paint curlicues extending from the leaves. Let dry completely.

5 *See illustration* to fold tongue of each shoe over toe, and center and glue between leaves. Basecoat flower petals with antique gold and shade 1 side of each petal with burnt sienna. Add highlights to tips of petals with cream.

6 *Basecoat center* of the sunflower with burnt umber. Paint black dots in center and dot outer edges with burnt umber and antique gold. Let dry. If desired, use the liner brush and black to print "Sunflowers" on each side of heel.

SHOE PATTERN

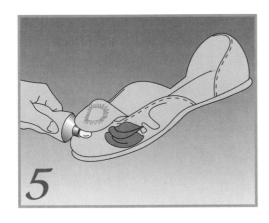
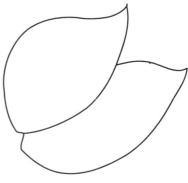
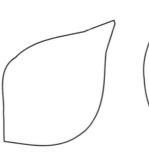

Tongue

𝓑allerina
BEAR

This sock doll stands 15" (38 cm) tall and is sewn from nylon anklets. She wears a no-sew tutu with ribbon and lace frills. Her toes, weighted with pellets, let her pirouette almost unassisted if her arms are supported. She will surely dance her way into the heart of every little ballerina.

LIST of MATERIALS

* White nylon anklet socks, one pair
* 4" (10 cm) white/pink self-gathering lace, 1⅓ yds. (1.27 m)
* 1½" (3.8 cm) pink satin ribbon, ⅓ yd. (0.32 m)
* 3/16" (4.5 mm) picot edge raspberry ribbon, 1 yd. (0.95 m)
* ⅞" (2.2 cm) white pleated satin ribbon, ⅓ yd. (0.32 m)
* ⅛" (3 mm) flat metallic pink ribbon, 1¼ yds. (1.15 m)
* ⅝" (1.5 cm) pink satin rose
* Polyester fiberfill

* Polypropylene mini pellets
* ⅜" (1 cm) flat lavender buttons, two
* ½" (1.3 cm) pink heart-shaped shank button
* Threads: white sewing, clear nylon upholstery
* Sewing needles: soft-sculpture, fine sewing
* Air-soluble marker
* Heavy-duty adhesive glue
* Miscellaneous items: scissors, tape measure, sewing machine (optional)

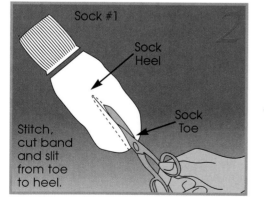

Sock #1
Sock Heel
Sock Toe
Stitch, cut band and slit from toe to heel.

1 *Stitching:* Stitch sock material, unless otherwise indicated, by hand or machine, right sides together, using a ⅛" (3 mm) seam allowance.

2 *Body & Legs:* Refer to the Step 2 illustration to turn Sock #1 inside out and stitch together from toe to heel for legs. Cut off the sock cuff, and slit in center of stitching for legs. Run 2 parallel lines of basting stitches around upper cut edge. Turn sock right side out; fill feet with pellets and stuff legs and body with fiberfill. Pull threads to close opening and whipstitch edges shut with upholstery thread.

3 *Arms:* Refer to the Step 3 illustration to cut off the toe section of Sock #2 for arms. Turn toe section inside out and stitch 2 tube shapes with rounded ends for arms. Cut apart, turn each arm right side out and stuff with fiberfill. Baste around upper opening edges; pull threads to close. Knot thread; push gathers to inside.

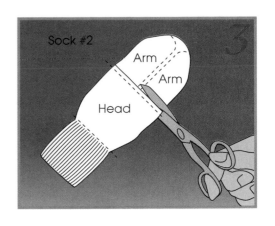

4 *Head:* Turn rest of sock inside out and stitch cut edges together. Run a line of basting stitches around sock where ribbed band begins. Turn and stuff with fiberfill. Heel will form face. Pull a basting thread to close and form neck; wrap thread around neck several times and knot. Fold cuff up over head, position head on body and tack together.

5 *Leotard:* Pull cuff down over body and tack edges together between legs. Tack an arm to each side of neck.

6 *Ears & Face:* Pinch off ears on each side of upper head, referring to photo. Stitch across pinch lines. Mark eyes, nose and mouth with marker. Thread soft-sculpture needle with upholstery thread, and insert at center back neck. See illustration stitch (1). Come up through mouth mark (2), take a tiny stitch (3), and reinsert needle to neck back (4). Pull thread to form a dimpled mouth. Repeat to stitch on lavender buttons for eyes and heart button for nose with white doubled thread; see illustration stitches (5-12).

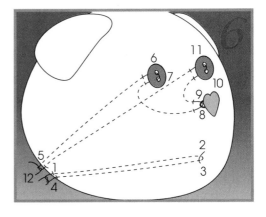

7 *Tutu:* Wrap the wide pink satin ribbon around torso under arms. Overlap in back, glue and trim excess. Repeat, gluing pleated white ribbon around neck. Place self-gathering lace around waist and pull gathering cord tight. Adjust gathers, tie knot, and trim. Glue lace to pink bodice lower edge.

8 *Finishing:* Cut 6" (15 cm) of pink picot edge ribbon and spot-glue center to front neck. Wrap ends around neck, overlap in back, and glue. Glue rose to front of ribbon. Tie remaining picot edge ribbon around head; make a bow in the front. Cut metallic ribbon in half. Wrap each piece around feet as shown in photo, beginning at ankles and tying knot at top below knees.

Watermelon
SERVING SET

Who would go to the hardware store for a serving set? A crafter, of course! This salad bowl, server and napkin rings began as a terra-cotta saucer for a flower pot, a garden tool and a length of PVC pipe. With a little paint and imagination, it's the perfect set to serve a summer salad on the patio!

LIST of MATERIALS

* 12½" (31.8 cm) terra-cotta saucer
* Wood handle garden trowel
* 1½" (3.8 cm) diameter PVC pipe, 1½" (3.8 cm) length per napkin ring
* Acrylic paints: buttermilk, dark green, black green, forest green, bright green, berry red, brandy wine, black

* Paintbrushes: Nos. 2, 12, and 20 flat; No. 1 liner; 1" (2.5 cm) sponge
* Nontoxic waterbase varnish
* Hot glue gun
* Small white silk flowers with leaves (optional)
* Miscellaneous items: disposable palette, water container, kitchen sponge, scissors, fine sandpaper, saw

TIPS and IDEAS

* Find watermelon print napkins to match the serving set, or some fabric to make your own. All you do is cut 18" (46 cm) squares, and hem or fringe the edges.
* This same idea could be done with many themes—soccer balls and sunshine, or pumpkins, oranges and tomatoes
* Use ceramic paints to make this set dishwasher safe.

1 *Preparation:* Sand the saucer and trowel handle to remove rough spots. Wash with warm water; do not use detergent or glass cleaner. Let dry thoroughly. See Step 1 illustration to cut PVC pipe into 1½" (3.8 cm) lengths. Sand well to remove lettering or oily residue. Wash thoroughly and let dry.

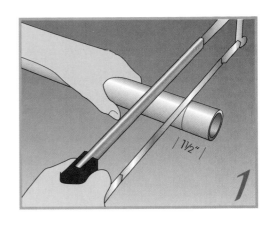

2 *Painting:* Refer to page 156 for Painting Instructions and Techniques. Basecoat outside of saucer with dark green. To sponge paint, cut corner of kitchen sponge. Wet sponge and squeeze dry. Pull corners up so center of sponge forms rounded pouf. Squeeze forest green and black green onto palette. Sponge outside of saucer sparsely with forest then black green.

3 *Watermelon Rind:* See Step 3 illustration to use a short zigzag stroke and large brush to paint irregular lines with bright green, forming watermelon stripes. Refer to the photo and Step 2 to paint watermelon pattern on a smaller scale on napkin rings and trowel handle.

4 *Watermelon Fruit:* Basecoat inside of saucer with buttermilk. To achieve a soft blending of colors, dampen top 1½" (3.8 cm) of the saucer with more buttermilk paint as you work. Lightly blend buttermilk and bright green on your brush and paint the top ½" (1.3 cm) of the saucer. See the Step 4 illustration to sponge the inside of the saucer with berry red, working from the center out into the buttermilk to create soft edges and a lighter color. Leave ½" (1.3 cm) buttermilk around edges for rind. Sponge lightly over berry red with brandy wine.

5 *Seeds:* Paint black seeds in bottom of saucer with points toward center. Highlight with buttermilk.

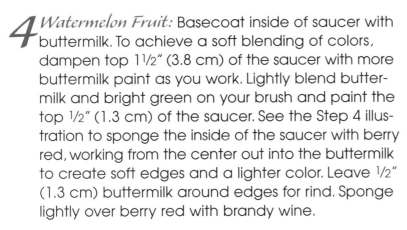

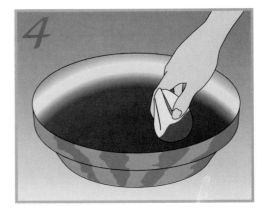

6 *Ladybug:* Underpaint the circle body with buttermilk. When dry, overpaint with berry red; 2 coats may be needed to cover. Refer to the photo to paint the head, feelers and spots with black. Pull a line of black along 1 side for a shadow. Let dry.

7 *Finishing:* Varnish each piece with several coats of nontoxic waterbase varnish. If desired, hot-glue small flowers and leaves to trowel handle and napkin rings. Refer to the photo for placement.

Mom's Recipe Book
& TEA JAR

This tea-time ensemble would make a great gift for the cook in your family, and is very easy to make. Fuse a purchased napkin to a memory book or photo album, and decorate with cotton molds and millefiori clay squares. If you can run a blender and cut a slice off a length of clay, you can do it!

LIST of MATERIALS

* 9" (23 cm) square memory book
* 16" (40.5 cm) square white and yellow gingham fringed napkin (or at least 7" (18 cm) bigger than memory book)
* 9" (23 cm) square double-sided fusible sheet adhesive
* Hot glue gun
* 2½" (6.5 cm) square terra-cotta Cotton Press® Tea Time mold*
* 1 sheet Cotton Press cotton linter paper and additive*
* Acrylic craft paint: blue, yellow, green
* Artist's brush

* Clear sheet of plastic
* 1 photo and 2 recipes
* Glass jar
* 2 pkgs. Friendly Clay™ millefiori canes: checkerboard/daisy design*
* Craft knife or razor blade
* Miscellaneous items: scissors, decorative-edge scissors, pencil, ruler, iron, oven, blender, fine-line blue marker, baking sheet lined with brown paper bag

*(See Sources on pg. 159 for purchasing information.)

TIPS and IDEAS

* You can decorate just about any container with millefiori clay canes, including ceramics, canisters, stoneware plates or pottery bean jars. Coordinate your choice with an appropriate terra-cotta mold design.

* An acid-free memory book is excellent for a recipe book because it is designed to be long-lasting and has a place for photos. That way you can include a snapshot of the recipe creator and the delicious end result.

RECIPE BOOK

1 Gingham Cover: Measure memory book cover; cut sheet adhesive to fit. Place napkin upside down on ironing board, and center adhesive on napkin. Follow manufacturer's instructions and fuse to napkin and then napkin to memory book cover. Fold 3" (7.5 cm) overlap up on each side, pressing folds as you go. Fold the overlap back over as shown in the illustration, so the fringe just hangs over the book; press fold on each side. Hot-glue 4 corners so they will not flip down.

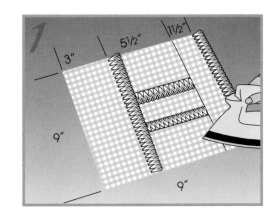

2 Cotton Molds: Cut 1½" x 2" (3.8 x 5 cm) of cotton linter; save. Follow manufacturer's instructions to make cotton pulp from rest of sheet. See illustration to pour pulp in mold. Make 2 complete molds and 3 frames with pulp only around outer edges. Adjust frame openings by gently ripping or cutting; trim ragged outer edges with scissors. When completely dry, paint the checkerboard blue, lemons yellow and leaves green.

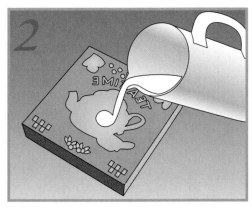

3 Assembly: Cut recipes and photo to fit frame openings. Cut plastic sheet into 3 pieces slightly smaller than frame outer edges. Place frames upside down on flat work surface, and hot-glue plastic sheets, recipes and photo upside down to frames. Hot-glue frames and 1 complete mold to recipe book cover. Use decorative-edge scissors to cut around saved piece, and print "Mom's Recipes" with marker; hot-glue to cover center.

4 Clay Squares: Follow manufacturer's instructions to cut 8 slices approximately ⅛" (3 mm) thick from clay canes using sharp craft knife. Place on baking sheet lined with paper and bake at 265°F (132°C) for 30 minutes. Cool, then hot-glue to cover as shown in photo.

TEA JAR

Follow instructions in Step 4 to cut enough clay squares to go around neck and lid of jar, plus 3 slices for jar sides. If jar lid has a plastic lining on the inner lid, **be sure to remove before baking.** See illustration to press slices around jar neck and lid firmly enough to adhere. Press slices together at seams to form 1 continuous band. Press 1 slice onto 3 sides of the jar. Place jar upright on baking sheet and bake as in Step 4. Cool jar; glue remaining mold to jar front.

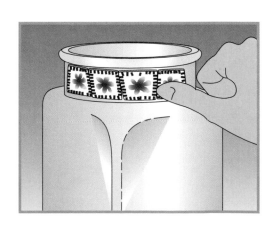

Picture-Perfect
MEMORIES

***R**elive happy times* from your vacation or a special event with a paper-layer photo picture! Two identical photos are cut, pieced together like a puzzle, accented with gold leaf paints, then set like tile on a mat board. Make one for yourself and another as a surprise gift for a friend!

LIST of MATERIALS

* Snapshot photo and two 8" x 10" (20.5 x 25.5 cm) color photocopy enlargements
* Clear gloss sealer
* Liquid gold leafing paint
* Paintbrushes: Nos. 4 and 12 flat
* 11" x 14" (28 x 35.5 cm) mounting board
* 11" x 14" (28 x 35.5 cm) mat with 7½" x 9½" (19.3 x 24.3 cm) opening, your color choice
* 11" x 14" (28 x 35.5 cm) frame, your choice
* White craft glue
* Spray adhesive (optional)
* Miscellaneous items: scissors, ruler or T-square, pencil, craft knife, 7" x 9" (18 x 23 cm) white posterboard, cutting surface, straightedge

TIPS and IDEAS

❋ Use a craft knife or rotary cutter to quickly and accurately cut the pieces.

❋ Use decorative scissors for special edge effects.

❋ Use greeting cards instead of photos.

1 *Trim photocopies* to measure 7" x 9" (18 x 23 cm). Glue back of 1 color copy to posterboard. Let dry, and trim if necessary. Spray adhesive may be used for mounting.

2 *Refer to the Step 2 Illustration* to measure and draw a grid on the back of both photocopies. Cut mounted copy along solid lines into 12 squares and 18 border pieces. Position each piece, faceup, in order of original photo.

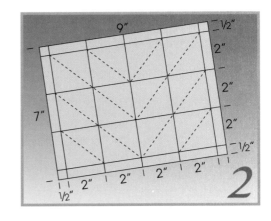

3 *Brush gold leaf paint* on the edge of each piece. Hold brush perpendicular to edge and pull downward for a more ragged look; let dry. See Step 3 illustration.

4 *Apply 2 coats* of sealer to each piece, letting dry between coats.

5 *Align the mat* over the mounting board, and glue. Center and glue the mounted pieces in the mat board opening, leaving ⅛" (3 mm) space between each piece.

6 *From second photocopy,* cut out only the 2" (5 cm) squares. Refer to the dashed lines in the Step 2 illustration to fold into triangles, wrong sides together. See the Step 6 illustration to glue opposite corners, but do not crease folds.

7 *Repeat Steps 3 and 4* to paint the nonfolded edges of the triangles and apply sealer.

8 *Refer to the Step 2 illustration* to glue the triangles in proper direction over the matching squares. Mount the layered photo and mat in a frame.

Springtime Bloom
ARRANGEMENT

Spring is the perfect time of year to perk up your home with a new flower arrangement—the colorful and graceful blossoms are so easy to work with. This simple design concept can be adapted for fresh, silk or dried flowers. If using fresh flowers, simply purchase the appropriate floral foam, and begin arranging.

* Silk flowers: three white lily 3-flower sprays; five yellow daffodils; six each forsythia branches, grass sprays, and 6" (15 cm) ivy sprigs
* 5" (12.5 cm) dried mushrooms, two
* Spanish moss
* Dried floral foam to fit container
* 3" (7.5 cm) spring floral wire-edge ribbon, 1½ yds. (1.4 m)

* 9" x 5" x 2" (23 x 12.5 x 5 cm) low ceramic container
* 2½" (6.5 cm) wood pick
* Hot glue gun
* Floral tape
* 16-gauge stem wire
* Miscellaneous items: wire cutters, craft knife, tape measure

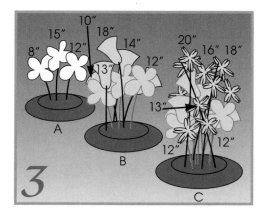

1 *Foam:* Cut with craft knife to fit container, being careful not to extend above rim. Hot-glue in place.

2 *Flower Stems:* Cut as follows, lengthening stems where necessary by adding wire and wrapping with floral tape:
  Lilies: 15" (38 cm), 12" (30.5 cm), 8" (20.5 cm)
  Daffodils: 18" (46 cm), 14" (35.5 cm), 13" (33 cm), 12" (30.5 cm), 10" (25.5 cm)
  Forsythia: 20" (51 cm), 18" (46 cm), 16" (40.5 cm), 13" (33 cm), 12" (30.5 cm), 12" (30.5 cm)

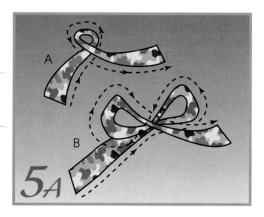

3 *Inserting Flowers:* Refer to the Step 3 illustration to insert flowers into foam. Start with 3 lilies (A), add 5 daffodils (B) and fill in with forsythia (C). All flowers (except ivy) are inserted straight into foam to create a vertical design. Mold, sculpt and bend each flower to give dimension and life.

4 *Mushroom Pieces:* Glue to right side of arrangement almost extending over edge of container and extending beyond line of flowers.

5 *Ribbon Bow:* Refer to the Step 5 illustrations to make bow from floral ribbon. Using ½ yd. (0.5 m), make a single loop with 7" (18 cm) tails. Using 1 yd. (0.95 m), make 2 single loops with 1 tail slightly longer. Tie single loop to center of double loop. Attach bow to wood pick and insert into left front of arrangement. Arrange loops under flowers and long tails over side edges of container. Arrange the 2 shorter tails of looped center to gracefully follow line of flowers and extend over edge of container. Spot-glue tails to container.

6 *Finishing:* See the photo to fill base of arrangement with ivy sprigs. Insert 2 in back and some peeking out from under bow and extending over sides of container.

*M*ade with a *variety of papers* and

ribbons, stamps with rainbow-colored inks, laces, charms and braids, this sentimental keepsake book is as beautiful as the memories it guards. For a graduate it can record autographs of friends and teachers; or capture the memories of other special occasions—weddings, anniversaries and birthdays.

LIST of MATERIALS

* Victorian rubber stamps, 2-5 designs
* Rainbow stamp pad
* 140 lb. (63 kg) acid-free white watercolor paper, 10" x 13" (25.5 x 33 cm)
* Heavyweight acid-free paper: assorted colors, 10" x 13" (25.5 x 33 cm), five sheets; dusty rose, 5¾" x 9" (14.5 x 23 cm), one sheet
* Acid-free parchment paper, 10" x 13" (25.5 x 33 cm), two sheets
* Cream mat board, 5" x 7" (12.5 x 18 cm)
* Ecru lace, 6" x 8" (15 x 20.5 cm)

* ⅛" (3 mm) silk or satin ribbon: dusty rose, ecru, burgundy, 1 yd. (0.95 m) each; white, blue, 1½ yds. (1.4 m) each
* Rose satin cord, ½ yd. (0.5 m)
* Thin gold cord, ⅔ yd. (0.63 m)
* Ribbon roses: ⅜" (1 cm) with leaves; 1"-2" (2.5-5 cm), two
* 4 gold charms
* 6 mm to 10 mm beads, five
* 6" (15 cm) paper heart doily
* Thick craft glue
* Glue gun
* Miscellaneous items: scissors, tape measure, pencil with eraser, darning needle

1 *Book Cover:* Fold watercolor paper in half crosswise. Trace the patterns on the next page and cut from mat board and lace as indicated. Center and glue dusty rose paper and lace heart to cover front.

2 *Ribbon Streamers:* Cut white and blue ribbon in half. Take each blue and white ribbon piece, and dusty rose and ecru, and tie into a bow with 3″ (7.5 cm) loops and uneven ends. Glue bow to lace, 1/2″ (1.3 cm) below center of book front. Randomly string and tie beads and charms on ribbon streamers. Center and glue mat board heart over bow.

3 *Stamping:* Stamp a rainbow ink design in the center of mat board heart, above the lace heart, and in each lower corner. Press the eraser end of a pencil on stamp pad and add ink dots around cover edges, as shown in Step 3 illustration.

4 *Embellishing:* Glue rose satin cord around edge of mat board heart. Glue a small ribbon rose to center top and 2 large ribbon roses to bottom heart.

5 *Book Pages:* Layer heavyweight and parchment papers in desired order with edges even. Fold in half and place inside cover. Open book to center page. Measure 3″ (7.5 cm) from top and bottom edges and mark center crease with X's.

6 *Binding:* Thread white, blue, and burgundy ribbons onto darning needle. With ribbon ends inside book, sew through fold at X's. Knot ribbon to hold pages securely together, letting ends dangle below bottom edge of book. Glue heart doily to an inside page and stamp pages as desired.

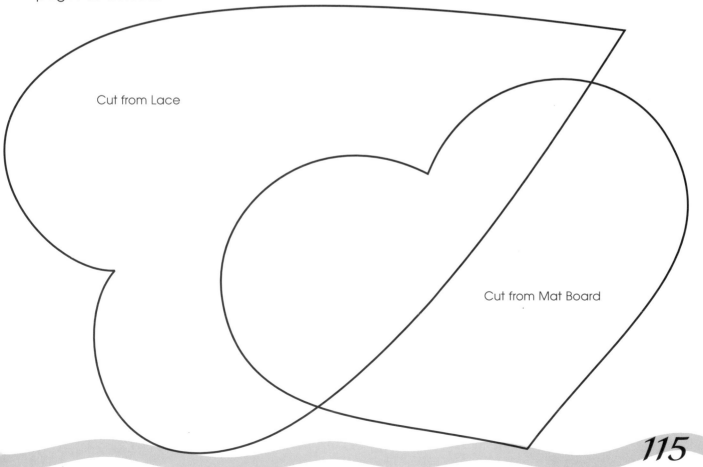

Cut from Lace

Cut from Mat Board

Appliqué
GOLF SHIRT & VISOR

The most avid golfer will be ready to swing into action dressed in this sporty shirt topped with matching visor cap. The comfy T-shirt takes on a designer look with letters appliquéd in coordinating fabrics. You don't have to be a painter to paint the faux golf ball with easy-to-use iridescent and liquid glitter paints. Matching bias binding trims the tee and purchased visor for a finishing touch that tops it off in style!

LIST of MATERIALS

* White T-shirt
* Purchased black fabric visor
* 45" (115 cm) coordinating cotton fabrics: ⅓ yd. (0.32 m) gingham; 4" (10 cm) square each, three calicoes
* ¼ yd. (0.25 m) paper-backed fusible web
* Fabric paints: dimensional charcoal iridescent, metallic midnight onyx, clear ice iridescent liquid glitter

* No. 8 flat paintbrush
* Fabric glue
* 20 mm black acrylic stone
* Pattern Sheet
* Miscellaneous items: scissors, ruler, T-shirt board, tracing paper, pencil, straight pins, sewing needle and matching thread, black permanent marker, press cloth, iron, sewing machine

❋ Host a crafting party and teach league members how to make this shirt for your official garb for the season.

❋ Change the wording and ball to your favorite pastime: CHOIR with a musical note in the O, for example.

1 *Preparation:* Wash and dry T-shirt and fabrics without using fabric softener; press.

2 *Gingham Bias Trim:* Cut four 3" x 18" (7.5 x 46 cm) bias gingham strips. With right sides together, sew short ends to make one 45" (115 cm) strip. This will be enough for shirt neckline and visor bow. Fold strip lengthwise with right sides together and sew a 1/8" (3 mm) seam. Turn to right side and press. Trim ends.

3 *Stitching:* Begin at center back of shirt neck to sew bias trim, seam edge down, to inside of neckband seam, overlapping and turning in ends. Fold and stitch over neckband on outside; see illustration.

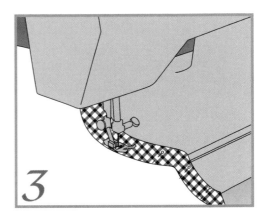

4 *Appliqués:* Trace the patterns. Fuse web to back of calicoes, and to a 5" (12.5 cm) gingham square. Refer to the photo to transfer letters to appropriate fabrics. Fuse letters to shirt front.

5 *Outlining:* Slip shirt onto T-shirt board and pin excess shirt to back. Outline raw edges of letters with charcoal iridescent paint, as shown in Step 5 illustration.

6 *Golf Ball:* Refer to the photo and use black marker to dot dimples on ball. See Side Loading Technique on page 156 to load corner of brush with midnight onyx and paint a graduated shadow on lower curve of ball. When barely dry to the touch, apply clear ice glitter to entire ball.

7 *Visor Bow:* Cut one 3" (7.5 cm) and two 9" (23 cm) lengths of bias trim. On one 9" (23 cm) length, turn in raw ends at a slight angle; glue ends. On remaining 9" (23 cm) length, overlap and glue ends. Center over the first 9" (23 cm) piece. See Step 7 illustration to wrap and glue 3" (7.5 cm) length around center. Glue black stone in center. Glue bow to visor.

Classic WINDOW

Stained glass is an old art form, and to do it well takes much practice and training. There is an easier version that comes very close to the look of real stained glass; but it uses paints. This design harks back to simpler times with a monochromatic color scheme emphasized by textured and frosted clear glass. Add the right frame, hang against a window, and you've got a classic that will make many people think it's an antique.

LIST of MATERIALS

* Styrene blanks* or 8" x 10" (20.5 x 25.5 cm) piece of glass
* 1 bottle Gallery Glass liquid leading*
* 1 bottle each Gallery Glass window colors*: crystal clear, amber, clear frost
* 1 medium flat artist's brush
* Pattern Sheet
* Miscellaneous items: tracing paper, red pencil, masking tape, paint palette, wooden toothpick or metal nut pick, cardboard piece 9" x 12" (23 x 30.5 cm) or larger, cotton swabs, craft knife
* *(See Sources on pg. 159 for purchasing information.)

1 **Preparation:** Trace pattern with red pencil to tracing paper; tape traced pattern to cardboard and place on a flat and level work surface. The cardboard will enable you to turn the project without moving the plastic or glass. Remove cover from styrene plastic or thoroughly clean both sides of glass. Tape plastic or glass over pattern.

2 **Leading:** See the Step 2 illustration to trace over solid lines on the pattern with the liquid leading, following manufacturer's instructions. Make sure that all lead lines are joined to prevent paint colors from seeping through. To correct mistakes, lift off wet leading with a cotton swab, or cut out dry leading with a craft knife.

3 **Coloring:** Fill in areas on the pattern according to the Color Key and the following instructions:
   #81—Apply crystal clear paint from the bottle in a scribbling motion. Do not comb.
   #22—Apply a thin layer of crystal frost paint with the artist's brush.
   #20—Apply amber paint from the bottle, and comb the area with a toothpick or nut pick.
   #22 and #81 in an area together—Fill in clear frost paint where shown on the pattern in the circles. Then fill rest of the area with crystal clear paint; swirl the 2 paints together with a toothpick or nut pick.

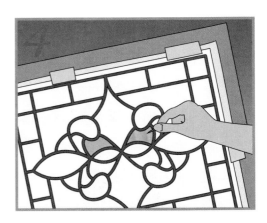

4 **Combing:** This is a technique used in Coloring which helps give a smooth texture to the paint and also helps remove air bubbles; see the Step 4 illustration.

5 **Finishing:** Tap plastic or glass from the bottom, after all coloring is done, to remove very stubborn bubbles, as shown in the Step 5 illustration. Let dry flat and undisturbed for 24 hours. Mat and frame as desired.

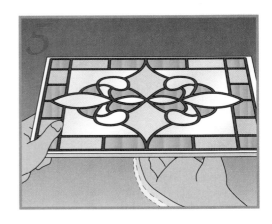

Dish Towel
PILLOW

Dish towels like these are just too pretty to use. But instead of hiding them away in a drawer, get them out and start crafting. Trimmed with Battenberg lace doilies, ribbons, buttons and yo yos, they can be whisked out of the kitchen and into the living room.

LIST of MATERIALS

* Fabric glue
* 14" (35.5 cm) square pillow form, one
* Coordinating plaid woven cotton dish towels, at least 17" x 29" (43 x 73.5 cm), one each: dark hunter, light hunter, light cranberry*
* Fabric/Battenberg doilies: one 4" (10 cm) cranberry square, one 5" (12.5 cm) dark green three-leaf holly cluster*
* 1½" (3.8 cm) gold print yo yo*, one
* 9" x 12" (23 x 30.5 cm) cream felt sheet
* ¼ yd. (0.25 m) lightweight fusible web
* ⅝" (1.5 cm) cranberry grosgrain ribbon, 6" (15 cm)
* Flat buttons: six 1" (2.5 cm) wood, one ⅜" (1 cm) dark for bird's eye
* Embroidery floss: cranberry, cream, hunter green
* Pattern Sheet
* Miscellaneous items: pencil, tracing and tissue paper, scissors, ruler, straight pins, iron, sewing machine and matching threads
* (See Sources on pg. 159 for purchasing information.)

1 *Preparation:* Cut a 4" x 5" (10 x 12.5 cm) cranberry rectangle and a 6" (15 cm) dark hunter square from the towels. Fuse web to wrong sides.

2 *Patterns:* Trace the bird and birdhouse patterns and cut from fused towel pieces. Place the birdhouse on the square doily as shown in photo. Trim doily edges to fit under birdhouse.

3 *Bird & Birdhouse:* See the Step 3 illustration to glue the grosgrain ribbon to the felt 2¾" (7 cm) from left short edge for the birdhouse pole, then trimmed cranberry doily to top of the ribbon. Refer to the photo to fuse the birdhouse on the doily, then the bird to lower right felt corner.

4 *Embroidery:* Refer to Embroidery Stitches on page 155 to blanket stitch edges of the house with cream floss and bird with cranberry. Sew ⅜" (1 cm) button eye to the bird. Trace the lettering pattern onto tissue paper and pin to the felt above the bird. Embroider lettering working ¼" (6 mm) hunter green running stitches. Carefully tear away tissue paper.

5 *Assembly:* Place the towel right side up; center the felt sheet. Pin felt to pillow and use cranberry floss to embroider diagonal straight stitches along edges as shown in the Step 5 illustration. Fold the towel inside out around the pillow and pin a center back seam. Stitch seam, turn right side out, and insert pillow form.

6 *Finishing:* Sew 3 buttons evenly spaced on each side of the pillow 2¼" (6 cm) from edges using green floss and tying knots on the front. Trim the floss leaving 1" (2.5 cm) tails. Refer to page 158 for instructions on how to make a yo yo, or use a premade yo yo. Glue yo yo to center of birdhouse for opening and the holly cluster to bottom of ribbon pole.

Butterflies'
HOME SWEET HOME

Paint a cozy habitat for your winged friends. Butterfly houses provide a substitute for the natural homes of these lovely creatures who share our world. Purchase premade houses or kits and use the pattern provided to paint posies as delicate and colorful as the butterflies we all enjoy.

LIST of MATERIALS

* Wood butterfly house: 3½" x 5" x 14" (9 x 12.5 x 35.5 cm)
* Acrylic paints: adobe, sage, medium blue, light blue, peach, butter cream, black, dark green
* Paintbrushes: Nos. 4 and 8 flat, No. 1 liner, old stencil brush
* Waterbase sealer
* Matte varnish
* Pattern Sheet
* Miscellaneous items: sandpaper, tack cloth, pencil, tracing paper, graphite paper, stylus, brush basin, disposable palette, paper towels

TIPS and IDEAS

* Not so great with a liner brush? Use a permanent-ink waterproof fine-line marker and draw those thin little lines.
* Don't paint the design at all—get a rub-on transfer.

1 *Preparation:* Refer to page 156 for Painting Instructions and Techniques. Sand all wood surfaces and wipe them with a tack cloth. Apply the sealer. Let dry between coats.

2 *Basecoat & Pattern:* Use the No. 8 brush to basecoat the entire house with adobe. Trace the pattern and use the graphite paper and a stylus to transfer to butterfly house front as shown in Step 2 illustration. Do not transfer the detail lines to the flowers, leaves and butterfly at this time.

3 *Painting:* See the Step 3 illustration and use the No. 4 brush to basecoat the following: oval flowers with medium blue; leaves, roof and slot opening inner edges with sage; butterfly wings and flat petal flowers with light blue; butterfly body and round petal flowers with peach; flower centers with butter cream.

4 *Details:* Transfer all details as done in Step 2. Refer to the photo to shade the leaves near the flower cluster with dark green. Use the liner brush to outline all pattern lines and stitches with black; see the Step 4 illustration. Float the outside edge of the butterfly wings with medium blue.

5 *Flyspecking:* Thin dark green to an inky consistency. Load an old stencil brush by dipping the bristles in paint. Practice spattering on a paper towel by pulling your thumbnail over the bristles to spatter the paint in varying-size dots. Lightly speckle the house. Apply several coats of varnish.

*S*ummertime
CLASSIC HATBAND

D*ress up a straw hat* with an elegant hatband ornament stitched on plastic canvas. Keep cool in the sun while you wear your new hat to the beach, boating or out for a walk. You can also use it as a belt to accessorize a new dress. Whatever the fashion, you will be in style!

LIST of MATERIALS

* 10-mesh plastic canvas, 1/4 sheet
* No. 20 tapestry needle
* DMC 6-strand embroidery floss listed on Color Key: 1 skein ivory, 2 skeins each pink and lavender
* Kreinik: aqua No. 32 heavy braid, 5 yds. (4.6 m); rainbow No. 8 fine braid, 8 yds.

* (7.35 m); 1/8" (3 mm) ivory ribbon, 7 yds. (6.4 m)
* 3 yds. (2.75 m) craft cord, white/gold
* 25 pearl pebble beads
* Wide brim straw hat
* Chiffon rectangular scarf, your choice
* Miscellaneous items: scissors, craft knife

1 *Refer to page 158* for Plastic Canvas General Instructions and Stitches. Use scissors to cut a 73x30-bar piece of canvas. Trim carefully following the bold outline on the Chart. Use the craft knife to cut out slots as indicated.

2 *Work continental stitches*, filling in each area with designated color. At the same time, overcast the slots with the adjacent color. Work slanting Gobelin stitches within area inside beads. Use 12 strands of floss to work the pink and lavender stitches. Use the 1/8" (3 mm) ivory ribbon for the areas marked ivory and the aqua braid for the areas marked aqua. Backstitch around each color area with rainbow braid and overcast outer edge with white/gold cord.

3 *To attach beads*, thread needle with 6 strands of ivory floss and work beaded half cross stitches. To anchor the beads, run the floss back through the entire chain of beads, and knot. Run scarf through the slots and tie hatband around hat.

COLOR KEY

Name	DMC
Ivory	1/8" Ribbon
Aqua Braid	014
Pink	3609
Lavender	340
Rainbow Backstitches	664
Bead	------

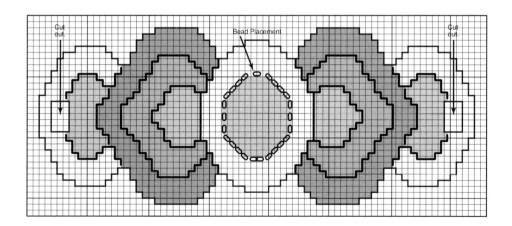

Quick!

Who says you can't teach an old dog new tricks? A lamp, painted tablerunner and quilts go much more quickly with a premade birdhouse base, stamped design, stencils and cheat sheets for piecing. The basket bouquet on the curtain rod shelf only looks painted—it is done with colored pencils and a

woodburner—and the tissue box layers are stitched with beads and pearl cotton. Even experienced crafters will love these and other updated techniques and new ideas that get the job done faster without losing any of the beauty.

Paisley Penny
VEST

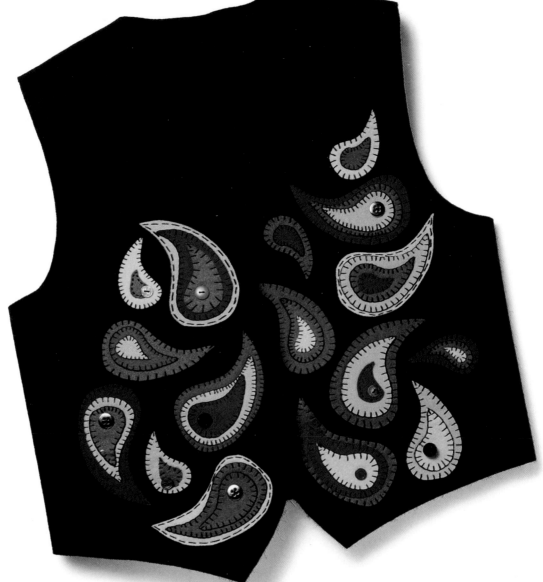

***N**ot made of just ordinary felt,* this vest is made of WoolFelt®, a fabric that is 35% wool and 65% rayon. It is soft and easy to work with, and because the edges don't ravel, you don't have to worry about finishing. Traditional Penny Rug designs provide the inspiration for the paisley pattern—arrange and layer the designs however you choose, creating depth and dimension with ever smaller layers.

LIST of MATERIALS

* ❋ Black presewn WoolFelt vest*
* ❋ Two 9" x 12" (23 x 30.5 cm) WoolFelt squares* each of: green, blue, red, orange, gold. (If you choose to embellish the back of your vest also, purchase ¼ yd. (0.25 m) of each color.)
* ❋ 1 skein 6-strand black embroidery floss
* ❋ 9 buttons, or other embellishments
* ❋ Pattern Sheet
* ❋ Miscellaneous items: tracing paper, pencil, scissors, sewing needle, straight pins
* *(See Sources on pg. 159 for purchasing information.)

* If you don't have the time right now to embroider the designs in place, use fabric glue or even fuse them onto the vest and each other. Add more buttons for embellishments, or embroider only the top design on each stack.

* Here might be your chance to try out all those embroidery stitches on your sewing machine! Machine-embroider the designs onto the vest, instead of doing it by hand; just do them in reverse. Start with the top paisley design onto the next, and so on down, until you machine-embroider the base paisley design onto the vest.

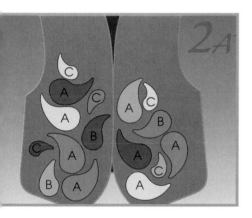

1 Preparation & Cutting: Trace 5 paisley patterns to tracing paper. Cut 44 paisley designs from the fabrics as follows:

    A: 1 green, 2 red, 1 orange, 2 gold, 2 blue
    B: 5 green, 2 red, 1 orange, 3 blue
    C: 2 green, 2 red, 2 orange, 4 gold, 5 blue
    D: 1 green, 3 red, 1 orange, 2 gold, 2 blue
    E: 1 blue

2 Stitching: Refer to the photo and Illustration 2A to begin layering the paisley designs onto the vest. Begin with the 8 A shapes, and then the other base paisley designs. Pin in place, and glue, fuse or embroider on with blanket or running stitches. Refer to page 157 for Embroidery Stitches. Add successive layers, stitching only through the previous paisley design layer, until all the paisley designs are attached. See Illustration 2B.

3 Embellishing: Complete your vest by stitching on the buttons, and add any other desired embellishments. Because WoolFelt does not ravel, you do not have to line or finish the edges of the vest in any way. However, if you choose, you could line the vest, or finish the edges with a decorative braid, trim or cord.

Country Birdhouse
LAMP

*T*he perfect lighting solution

for a cozy nook in your home, this charming
lamp is sure to be a hit. A stenciled
checkerboard trim, crackle finish and a tin
lamp shade give it loads of country appeal.

LIST of MATERIALS

* Wood: 4" x 9" x 4" (10 x 23 x 10 cm) birdhouse*; 1½"
  (3.8 cm) leaves*, eight; 2½" (6.5 cm) bird; ¾" x 5½" (2
  x 14 cm) square for lamp base *(See Sources on pg.
  159 for purchasing information.)
* Wood primer
* Acrylic paints: medium poppy, deep blush, deep
  peach, deep sage, black, ivory
* Paintbrushes: ¾" (2 cm) flat, liner, small stencil
* Gel medium
* Crackle medium and activator
* ³⁄₁₆" (4.5 mm) checkerboard stencil
* Matte varnish
* 6½" x 9" (16.3 x 23 cm) tin duct lamp shade
* Lamp hardware
* White craft glue
* Miscellaneous items: sandpaper, tack cloth, small
  sponge, disposable palette, soft cloth

1 *Preparation:* Refer to page 156 for
Painting Instructions and Techniques.
Apply 1 coat of primer to all the wood
pieces. Let dry. Lightly sand each piece;
wipe with a tack cloth.

2 *Crackle Medium:* Follow manufacturer's instructions to apply crackle medium and ivory paint with the flat brush to the top of the roof, the birdhouse walls and the top of the lamp base.

3 *Painting:* Let dry between each paint coat, and paint over the crackle/ivory mix, if necessary. Paint the following deep sage: birdhouse roof, openings, pegs, birdhouse base, lamp base, wood leaves and lamp shade trim. Paint the lamp hardware stem, finial and the birdhouse walls deep peach, and the bird ivory.

4 *Checkerboard:* Position the checkerboard stencil on the lamp base sides and stencil the design deep peach.

5 *Crackling/Distressing:* If using a crackle medium activator, brush onto the top of the roof, the birdhouse walls and the lamp base. Lightly sand the edges of all the wood pieces as desired for a "distressed" look. Wipe the pieces with a tack cloth.

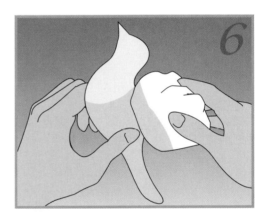

6 *Bird:* Mix 2 parts gel medium with 1 part deep peach paint. Brush the gel mix onto both sides and edge of the bird. See illustration to wipe off excess with a soft cloth. Use the liner brush to dot a black eye and to paint the beak deep blush.

7 *Leaves:* Lightly sponge the leaves with medium poppy and deep peach paint as desired.

8 *Gluing:* Glue the birdhouse to the center of the lamp base as shown in the illustration. Glue the leaves and the bird as desired to the birdhouse.

Lamp Base (upside down)

9 *Finishing:* Apply matte varnish to the entire lamp. Refer to the manufacturer's instructions to install the lamp hardware in the base and to attach the lamp shade.

Easy Triangle
SAMPLER QUILT

Everyone loves a quilt, but most of us just don't have the time to make one. A cheat sheet makes the triangle piecing on this quilt easy, and a simple border with no binding and machine quilting are two more ways to make this beauty as quickly as possible.

LIST of MATERIALS

✳ 45″ (115 cm) wide 100% cotton fabrics*: ½ yd. (0.5 m) hand-dyed pink for triangles, 1 yd. (0.95 m) burgundy print for triangles and borders, ½ yd. (0.5 m) green print for sashing, 1⅛ yd. (1.05 m) burgundy solid for backing

✳ 36″ (91.5 cm) square thin cotton/poly batting

✳ 3″ (7.5 cm) finished Half Square Triangle Paper™*

✳ Miscellaneous items: scissors, rotary cutter and cutting surface (optional), straight pins, sewing machine and matching threads, safety pins for basting

*(See Sources on pg. 159 for purchasing information.)

132

1 **Triangle–Squares:** Cut four 8½" x 16½" (21.8 x 41.8 cm) pieces each from pink and burgundy print. Place a piece of pink and burgundy right sides together. Pin Triangle Paper onto the fabrics in 4 corners and along dotted stitching lines. Repeat 3 more times. Follow Triangle Paper directions to stitch and cut; see the Step 1 illustration. Carefully tear off paper. Press seams toward burgundy fabric; trim points to make squares.

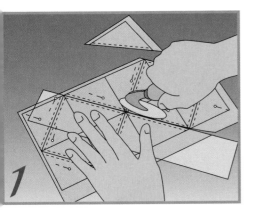

2 **Blocks:** Refer to photo to lay out triangle-squares into blocks. See the Step 2 illustration to stitch the squares together into 4 horizontal rows. Then stitch the 4 rows together, matching at seams, for a total of four 16-square blocks. Press seams to 1 side.

3 **Quilt Top:** Cut sashing strips from green fabric: two 2" x 12½" (5 x 31.8 cm) , three 2" x 26" (5 x 66 cm) and two 2" x 29" (5 x 73.5 cm). Stitch the 12½" (31.8 cm) strips between 2 blocks, making 2 horizontal rows. Stitch the 26" strips (66 cm) between the horizontal rows, and to the top and bottom edges; see the Step 3 illustration. Stitch the 29" (73.5 cm) strips to quilt-top sides.

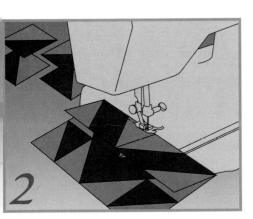

4 **Borders:** Measure quilt top across middle and cut 2 strips from burgundy print that length and 3" (7.5 cm) wide. Pin-mark border and quilt-top centers. Pin borders to quilt-top top and bottom edges, matching centers, and stitch. Repeat for side borders, measuring quilt top from top to bottom.

5 **Assembly:** Cut backing fabric in half along foldline. Stitch a seam where you just cut, right sides together, leaving an 8" (20.5 cm) opening near center. Press the seam open. Lay quilt top over backing, and trim excess backing fabric. Pin-mark centers of quilt top, backing and batting. Lay batting on flat surface, then quilt top faceup, and backing facedown. Match pin-marks, pin around all edges, and stitch a ¼" (6 mm) seam. Trim seam and corners.

6 **Quilting:** Turn quilt right side out through the opening in backing. Hand-stitch the opening shut; press quilt lightly. Pin-baste beginning in center; go up the middle, and then pin lines approximately every 5" (12.5 cm). Machine-quilt with a walking foot. Stitch in the ditch (in the seamlines) around triangles, and along sashing and border.

7 **Hanging Sleeve:** Refer to page 158 for instructions on how to make a hanging sleeve.

133

Stencil Shimmering
IVY BOXES

Stencils take on a whole new look when you go beyond paint alone. A simple ivy stencil turns to a work of art when combined with easy metallic foil. Dramatically different looks are achieved on these two boxes by choosing a variety of colors and hues.

LIST of MATERIALS

* For Each Box
* Ivy stencil
* Paintbrushes: ³/₈" (1 cm) stencil, 1" (2.5 cm) sponge brush
* Foil adhesive
* Foil sealer
* Thick white craft glue

For Green Ivy Box
* 9¹/₂" (24.3 cm) hexagon papier mâché box
* Stencil paint: hunter green, jungle green
* Silver foil sheet
* Acrylic paints: ivory, green sea, Christmas green
* 1 yd. (0.95 m) twisted cord, your choice

For Autumn Leaves Box
* 10" (25.5 cm) papier mâché box
* Gold foil sheet
* Brown velvet acrylic paint
* Stencil paint: amber, red, green
* Upholstery fabric, 5" x 36" (12.5 x 91.5 cm)
* 3 yd. (2.75 m) twisted cord, your choice
* Miscellaneous items: pencil, ruler, scissors, disposable palette

GREEN IVY BOX

1 Refer to page 156 for Painting Instructions and Techniques. Use the sponge brush and acrylic paints to basecoat the box lid top ivory, the box with green sea and lid side with Christmas green; let dry.

2 Place leaf stencil on box lid as shown in illustration. Use sponge brush to apply a very light coat of foil adhesive on the leaves by tapping brush up and down. Let dry until clear.

3 Follow manufacturer's instructions to press silver foil with fingers onto the adhesive-coated leaves. The bowl of a spoon or a wooden brush handle may also be used to burnish foil. Apply 1-2 coats of sealer to box lid.

4 *Position the stencil* over leaves. Use the stencil brush and 2 green shades of stencil paint to lightly paint the foiled leaves. Let some foil show through; let dry. Apply 1 or more coats of sealer. Glue cord around base of box.

AUTUMN LEAVES BOX

1 *Paint entire box brown,* including the inside. Let dry.

2 *Refer to Step 2 of Green Ivy Box* to place stencil on lid and apply adhesive on the leaves and around lid rim. Refer to Step 3 of Green Ivy Box to apply gold foil onto the leaves and lid rim, and apply sealer.

3 *Refer to the Step 3 illustration* to stencil the foiled leaves and lid rim with the amber, red and green stencil paint. Paint lightly so foil shows through; let dry. Apply 1 or more coats of sealer to painted areas.

4 *Place lid on box* and draw a pencil line around box where lid rim ends. Cut fabric to fit box below pencil line. Use the sponge brush to apply glue to box and smooth fabric in place. Glue cord around top rim of lid and around top and bottom fabric edges on box.

Cross-Stitched
FRONT DOOR

Display this cross-stitched front door in your entryway, changing its mini accents with the rebirth of each new season.

LIST of MATERIALS

- 28-count antique white even-weave fabric, 21" x 26" (53.5 x 66 cm)
- 14-count white perforated plastic, 8½" x 11" (21.8 x 28 cm)
- Anchor 6-strand embroidery floss in colors listed on Color Key, 1 skein each
- No. 24 tapestry needle
- 1/16" (1.5 mm) satin ribbon: ½ yd. (0.5 m) each red, pink; antique blue, ¼ yd. (0.25 m)
- 3/8" (1 cm) hook and loop fastener dots, eight
- Frame and mat, your choice
- Pattern Sheet
- Miscellaneous items: small sharp scissors, sewing needle, matching sewing thread, craft knife

1 *Front Door:* Refer to page 155 for Cross-Stitch Instructions and Techniques. Cross-stitch over 2 threads using 2 strands of floss. Begin by finding the center of the fabric. Count up and over to the top window where you will stitch your family name. Draw your name in the blank door chart using the alphabet. Adjust your name in the space accordingly. You may widen the top window to make more room for a longer name, if necessary. Stitch your name with Med. Linen 392. Then stitch the rest of the front door design.

2 *Backstitches:* Use a single strand of Dk. Brass 906 to work all backstitches.

3 *Seasonal Decorations:* Stitch using 2 strands of floss over 1 square of perforated plastic. Leave 2 or 3 spaces between each decoration; use small sharp scissors to cut out. Cut out wreath center using craft knife. With sewing needle and thread, stitch smooth fastener dots to door and step. Stitch other side of dots to each decoration back, checking placement. Refer to the photo to attach bows to decorations as follows: red on poinsettia garland; pink on spring wreath and straw hat; blue on sunflower broom.

COLOR KEY

Symbol	Name	Anchor
○	Ultra Light Carnation	23
◉	Light Blush	31
✛	Dark Blush	35
✬	Dark Blossom Pink	39
▲	Medium Emerald	227
△	Medium Spring Green	238
⊕	Medium Light Citrus	302
▣	Medium Topaz	307
■	Dark Topaz	309
◐	Medium Ecru	388
#	Medium Linen	392
▮	Dark Brass	906
♡	Ultra Light Antique Blue	1031
✱	Light Antique Blue	1033
◆	Medium Antique Blue	1034
—	Dark Brass Backstitches	906

FALL

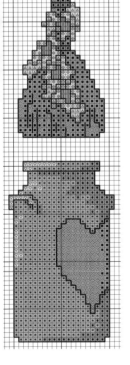

WINTER

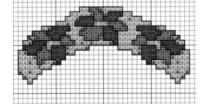

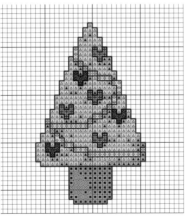

SPRING

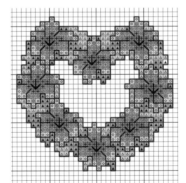

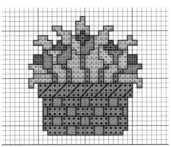

SUMMER

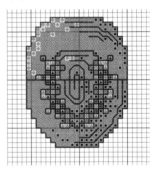

Basket Bouquet
QUILT RACK

If you loved color books when you were a child, then you'll love this fun and easy way of decorating wood. You outline the design with a woodburning tool, and then color it in with oil pencils. The pencils make wonderful shading and highlighting possible so you get a painted effect without ever picking up a brush.

LIST of MATERIALS

* ❋ 1 pine Quilt Rack/Curtain Rod*
* ❋ Graphite transfer paper
* ❋ Semigloss water-based varnish
* ❋ Paintbrushes: small sable artist's brush, large makeup or paintbrush
* ❋ Creative Woodburner with Cone Point tip*
* ❋ Oil pencils: clay rose, lt. blue, celadon green, white, lt. peach, neutral gray, burnt umber, dk. green, red violet, yellow*
* ❋ Oak wood stain
* ❋ Clear acrylic spray
* ❋ Pattern Sheet
* ❋ Miscellaneous items: tracing paper, pencil, tape, pencil sharpener, very fine sandpaper, tack cloth, red pencil, ruler, paper

*(See Sources on pg. 159 for purchasing information.)

1 *Preparation:* Lightly sand surface with grain; remove dust with tack cloth. Trace pattern onto tracing paper. Tape pattern at each corner centered on shelf. Work all steps with shelf facing you and pattern actually upside down. Cut graphite paper to fit behind pattern, and slide it under, graphite side down. Trace only the bold design lines with red pencil, not any shading or highlighting markings; don't press too hard. Remove pattern and graphite.

2 *Woodburning:* Place cone point in woodburner; follow manufacturer's instructions and cautions for use. Plug in and let heat for 5 minutes. Practice on scrap wood; use the burner just like a pencil. Do not use heavy pressure; let the heat do the work. Outline the entire design, working from 1 side to another as shown in Step 2 illustration. Make the lines dark enough so they will still show as wood ages.

3 *Color Layer 1:* Color in each item completely with the first color shown on the pattern. Color rose petals clay rose on the inner edge; blend into white on the outer edge. Use medium pressure and short back-and-forth strokes. Don't touch what you've colored because it will smear. Whisk away pencil crumbs with a large brush.

4 *Shading:* Refer to the photo and pattern and use burnt umber to shade with a medium pressure. Blend the shading, smudging the colors together with a finger. Shade in groupings, such as all daisies, the basket, and leaves. Place a plain piece of paper under your hands to avoid smearing.

5 *Highlighting:* Refer to slash lines on pattern and Step 5 illustration. Use a medium to heavy pressure with dk. green on the ivy leaves, white on the regular leaves and red violet on the outward and upward-facing rose petals. Blend the colors as in Step 4.

6 *Color Layer 2:* Color second color shown on the pattern. Use a heavy pressure and color completely over previous layers.

7 *Finishing:* Use small artist's brush to seal the colored design with the water-based varnish, as shown in illustration. Work slowly and stay inside the lines; do 2 coats for a glossy finish. Let dry completely before staining and sealing according to manufacturer's instructions.

Trip Around the World AFGHAN

Beautifully blended shades of blue and rose on a backdrop of pure white make this crocheted afghan a sight to behold. The quilt design will add a charming country touch to your home, and its generous size will make it extremely cozy to cuddle under during the cool fall and winter months.

LIST of MATERIALS

* 4-ply worsted weight acrylic yarn, 3.5-oz. (99 g) skeins: 6 white; 4 each medium blue, burgundy; 3 each pink, variegated, navy
* Size G crochet hook
* Miscellaneous items: scissors, ruler

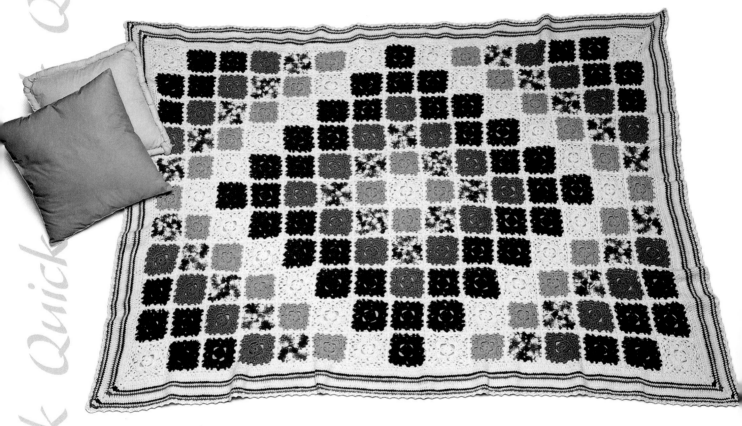

1 *General:* Refer to page 154 for Crochet Abbreviations and Stitches.
Gauge: Basic square measures 4½" (11.5 cm).
Squares Needed: 27 white, 26 pink, 28 variegated, 28 medium blue, 28 burgundy, 28 navy.

2 *Basic Square:* Ch 5, join with sl st to form ring.

Rnd 1: Ch 3 (first dc made), 2 dc in ring, *ch 2, 3 dc in same ring, rep from * around 3 times, ch 2, join with sl st to top of ch 3.

Rnd 2: *Ch 5, sc in ch-2 sp, rep from * around 3 times, join with sl st in first ch-5 sp.
Rnd 3: *Ch 3 (first dc made), 8 dc in ch-5 sp, sl st to next ch-5 sp, rep from * around 3 times (4 shells). Join with sl st to base of first ch 3.

Rnd 4: Ch 3, sc in each dc around square (32 loops). Join with sl st to first ch-3 loop.

Rnd 5: Ch 2 (first sc made), 2 sc in same sp, *ch 3, skip loop, sc in next loop, ch 3, skip loop, 3 sc, ch 2, 3 sc in corner, ch 3, skip loop, sc in next loop, ch-3, skip loop, 3 sc in next loop, rep from * around 3 times. (3 sc will be between 2 shells.) Ch 3, sl st to ch-2 to join. (See close-up photo of burgundy square below.)

3 *Square Border:* With white yarn, ch 3, sc in ch-3 sp, *ch 2, sc in next ch-3 sp, ch 2, 3 sc, ch 2, 3 sc in corner, ch 2, sc in next ch-2 sp, 3 sc in next sp, ch 2, 3 sc in next sp, rep from * around 3 times, join sl st to ch-3; fasten off.

4 *Joining Squares:* Refer to the illustration and photo and use white yarn to join squares. Begin with center square and slipstitch or sew square to each side. Continue around to outer edge.

COLOR KEY

☐	White	▨	Medium Blue
■	Pink	■	Burgundy
■	Variegated	■	Navy

5 *Border:*

Rnds 1–2: With white yarn, dc in each st around with 3 dc, ch 2, 3 dc in corner.

Rnd 3: With burgundy, sc in each dc with 3 sc, ch 2, 3 sc in each corner.

Rnd 4: Repeat Rnd 3 with white.

Rnd 5: Repeat Rnd 3 with medium blue.

Rnds 6–7: Repeat Rnd 1.

Rnd 8: Repeat Rnd 3.

Rnd 9: Repeat Rnd 4.

Rnd 10: Repeat Rnd 5.

Rnd 11: With white, *3 dc, ch 2, 3 dc, skip 1 sc, sc in next sc, skip next sc. Sc, dc, sc in next sc, rep from * across to next corner sp ending before last corner. Join with sl st to beg sl st. Fasten off. Weave in yarn ends.

*A**lthough these** grapes look good enough to eat, they don't take the talents of an artist to make them look real. They are stamped on with a decorator block, and the vines and curlicues lightly brushed on. Glue brass grape charms to brass rings, and you've got a coordinated table in a jiffy.*

LIST of MATERIALS

For Table Runner 18½" x 48" (47.3 x 122 cm)
* 1¼ yd. (1.15 m) off-white fabric
* ¼ yd. each (0.25 m) purple fabric and fusible interfacing
* Grapevine-motif decorator blocks or stamps*
* Decorator glazes or paints: purple, alpine green, ivy green, brown, mushroom, neutral*
* Artist's brushes: small round and small flat

For Napkin Rings
* Brass rings with 1½" (3.8 cm) inside diameter*
* Brass grape cluster charm charms*
* Amazing Goop® glue
* Brass cleaner and clear acrylic sealer, optional
* Miscellaneous items: scissors or rotary cutter and cutting surface, iron, measuring tape, pencil, masking tape, paint palette, straight pins, sewing machine and matching threads

*(See Sources on pg. 159 for purchasing information.)

TIPS and IDEAS

* Don't want to take the time to make a table runner? Simply purchase a solid-color runner, and start stamping.
* Decorator blocks and stamps come in just about any design imaginable. If you are the hostess with the mostest you can quickly create table linens of all kinds—placemats, napkins, tablecloths, runners—for any occasion, season or holiday.

NAPKIN RINGS

Follow brass-cleaner manufacturer's instructions to clean brass rings and grape charms. Seal brass surfaces to prevent tarnishing using clear acrylic sealer. Brass pieces can be left unsealed for a tarnished patina. Apply drop of glue to back of grape charm; press brass ring into glue. Prop ring up until glue is set by placing charm under large phone book, and leaning ring against side of book. Let dry completely.

TABLE RUNNER

1 **Preparation:** Wash and press fabrics; do not use fabric softener. Cut 23" x 45" (58.5 x 115 cm) from off-white fabric. Cut two 9" x 19½" (23 x 49.8 cm) pieces from purple fabric and two 4" x 18½" (10 x 46.3 cm) pieces from interfacing. Fold off-white fabric in half lengthwise and crosswise; place a small piece of tape at center. Tape fabric to a covered work surface. Place a tape guideline 3" (7.5 cm) in from short sides; keep stamps within tape; see Step 1 illustration.

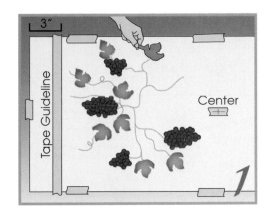

2 **Grapes:** Apply purple glaze to grape cluster stamp, not handle, with flat brush. Test on fabric scrap, following manufacturer's recommendations. Stamp in the middle of fabric, 4" (10 cm) below center. Stamp additional grapes to make a bunch 5" x 3" (12.5 x 7.5 cm). See Step 1 illustration.

3 **Vines:** Squeeze a small amount of mushroom, brown and neutral glazes next to each other on paint palette. Drag round wet brush through glazes. Refer to photo to paint vine upward from grape bunch, twisting brush between fingers as you paint. Paint vine again, using wet brush with no glaze. Split into a right and left vine; at the end of each, stamp additional grape bunches, 3½" x 2½" (9 x 6.5 cm).

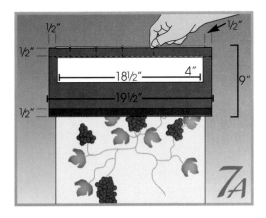

4 **Leaves:** Squeeze alpine green and ivy green glaze onto paint palette. Apply some of each color to leaf stamp, blending colors together; stamp leaf at desired location. Paint leaf stems same as vines in Step 3 above.

5 **Finishing Stamping:** Repeat Steps 3-5 to paint 2 grape bunches, vines and leaves on other side. Let paint dry. Heat-set paint, following manufacturer's instructions.

6 **Center Panel:** Cut stamped fabric to 19" x 41½" (48.5 x 105.5 cm), centering design. Cut backing from off-white fabric the same size. Pin the 2 pieces right sides together, and stitch ¼" (6 mm) seam along the 2 long edges. Press seam allowances open. Turn right side out; press. Baste across short open edges of center panel ⅜" (1 cm) from raw edges.

7 **Border:** Place interfacing fusible side down on wrong side of purple pieces, ½" (1.3 cm) from 1 long edge and the 2 short edges. Fuse, following manufacturer's instructions. Press up ½" (1.3 cm) to wrong side on opposite long edge. See Step 7A illustration to pin unpressed edge of border pieces to center panel ends, right sides together. Border pieces will extend ½" (1.3 cm) on each side. Stitch ½" (1.3 cm) seams; trim center panel seam allowance to ¼" (6 mm). Press seam toward border. Fold border piece in half lengthwise, right sides together, as shown in Step 7B illustration. Stitch ½" (1.3 cm) seam across sides; trim seam allowances. Turn border pieces right side out; press. Slipstitch openings closed; press.

Dimensional
TISSUE BOX

The dimensional design of this tissue box cover will have everyone asking "How did you do that?" It's easier than it looks. Simply cut and layer graduated pieces of plastic canvas and stitch through all the layers. A combination of light and dark pearl cotton threads provides a shading effect to emphasize the design.

LIST of MATERIALS

* 3¼ sheets 10-mesh ivory plastic canvas
* No. 3 pearl cotton: light salmon, medium salmon, light blue, medium blue, ivory
* ¹/₁₆" (1.5 mm) metallic gold ribbon
* No. 22 tapestry needle
* 6 mm round gold beads, 24
* Pattern Sheet
* Miscellaneous items: scissors, craft knife, emery board

1 *Cutting Box:* Refer to page 158 for Plastic Canvas Instructions and Stitches. Cut one 46x46-hole top and four 46x56-hole side panels. Cut the 12x12-hole top opening according to the bold outlines on the chart. Trim off nubs and trim the outside corners diagonally. Use the emery board to smooth the edges of the top opening.

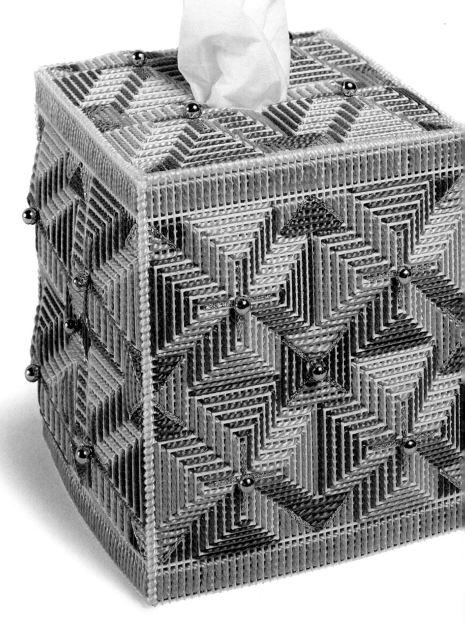

2 *Cutting Layer Pieces:* Cut 20 each of the following size squares: 21x21-hole, 19x19-hole, 17x17-hole, 15x15-hole, 13x13-hole, and 11x11-hole. Trim off the nubs **but do not cut** the corners diagonally. See Step 2 illustration to cut a 5x5-hole notch from each corner of each square.

3 *Stitching Instructions:* Follow the charts to work straight stitches using 1 strand of pearl cotton or metallic ribbon. To keep the ribbon stitches flat, do not let ribbon twist while stitching.

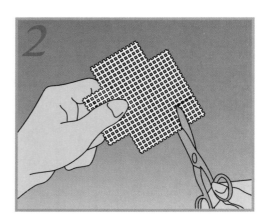

4 *Top Panel Salmon Stitches:* Place a 21x21-hole piece on the top panel. Start at the upper left corner with light salmon thread as shown in the illustration. Work a vertical stitch next to the first piece just through the top panel. Work the next vertical stitch through both the piece and the top panel. Place a 19x19-hole piece on top and work the next vertical stitch through both pieces and the panel. Continue adding smaller pieces, stitching through all the layers. Complete all light salmon stitches. Repeat to stitch the remaining 3 stacks of pieces. Work the dark salmon, stitching through all the layers.

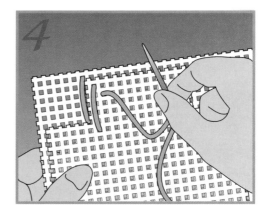

5 *Top Panel Blue Stitches:* Stitch the med. blue and lt. blue on the pieces and in the areas between. Work the diagonal stitches between the pieces and straight stitches on the top pieces with gold ribbon, attaching the beads as you stitch.

6 *Side Panels:* Repeat Steps 4 and 5 to stitch 4 pieces onto each side panel.

7 *Finishing:* Use ivory to overcast the sides together, and then attach the top to the sides.

Folk Dolls QUILT

Dolls stenciled on a quilt bring the charm of yesteryear into your home. Muslin used for the nine-block quilt is first tea-dyed for an antique look, then stenciled with dolls. Drape the quilt across an old doll cradle or display it as a wall hanging.

LIST of MATERIALS

* 45" (115 cm) miniprint cotton fabrics, ⅛ yd. (0.15 m) each, 10 assorted light and dark
* 45" (115 cm) natural muslin, 1⅛ yd. (1.05 m) (¾ yd. (0.7 m) for quilt back)
* 3 yd. (2.75 m) coordinating color piping
* 24" (61 cm) square batting

* Stencil plastic, 5½" (14 cm) squares, two
* Assorted acrylic paints to coordinate with fabrics
* Paintbrushes: No. 4 stencil, one for each paint color; fine liner
* Black fine-point permanent marker
* Pattern Sheet

* Miscellaneous items: tracing and typing paper, scissors, sewing machine and needles, matching sewing and ivory quilting threads, straight pins, tape measure, disposable palette, 3 tea bags, paper towels, masking tape, spray bottle filled with white vinegar, iron, craft knife, rotary cutter and mat (optional), fine sandpaper

1 ***Tea-Dyeing:*** Immerse fabric in a solution of 3 tea bags in 1 quart (1 L) of water for 3 mInutes; rinse in cold water. Wring out excess water and iron dry.

2 ***Patterns & Cutting:*** Trace the quilt patterns. Cut out fabric strips A-D as indicated. Also cut nine 5½" (14 cm) muslin squares.

3 ***Making Stencils:*** Place stencil plastic over the doll and dress stencil patterns and trace with marker. Place plastic on cutting surface and use craft knife to cut out.

4 *Stenciling:* Place muslin square on a piece of sandpaper; center and tape doll stencil onto muslin. Refer to page 156 and use Stippling Technique to paint body, being careful not to let paint seep beneath stencil. See the Step 4 illustration to shade body. Use a different brush for each paint color. Remove stencil and let dry. Tape dress stencil on doll, and stencil using your choice of paint. Use a darker paint color to shade along top, bottom and left dress edge; see Step 5 illustration. Dry-brush cheeks with red paint.

5 *Details:* Refer to the photo and use the fine liner brush or marker to paint curls around each doll head. Also paint or draw stripes, polka dots, etc., on each dress. Refer to the Step 5 illustration to draw mock stitch lines, ruffles and string bow on dress.

6 *Heat–Setting:* Spray each stenciled block with vinegar. Place a sheet of paper on block. Iron muslin dry, lifting paper occasionally to avoid sticking.

7 *Quilt Assembly:* Refer to the Step 7 illustration. Sew with 1/4" (6 mm) seams, right sides together. Press seams toward darker fabric. Stitch an A strip to left side of each muslin square, then a B strip to bottom edge. Stitch diagonal seam where A and B strips meet. Sew 3 blocks together to form a horizontal row, then 3 rows together. Stitch C strip to right edge of quilt and D strip to top edge. Stitch diagonal seam where C and D strips meet. Press quilt top.

8 *Basting:* Cut muslin backing and batting 2" to 4" (5 to 10 cm) larger than quilt top on each side. Pin-mark the center of each side for quilt top, backing and batting. Place quilt top, right side up and matching centers, on batting. Baste around entire quilt close to edge. Starting in a corner, sew piping around quilt top. Place backing on quilt top, right sides together and matching centers. Leave an opening to turn; sew along piping seam. Turn and slipstitch opening.

9 *Quilting:* Begin in center and work outward. Machine- or hand-quilt around each doll and 1/4" (6 mm) from all seams.

10 *Hanging Sleeve:* Refer to page 158 for instructions on how to make a hanging sleeve.

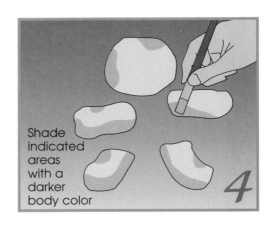

Shade indicated areas with a darker body color

4

5

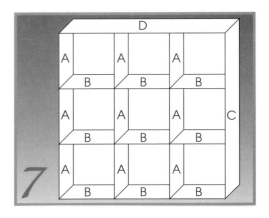

7

Painted Glass
BEVERAGE SET

Painting glass has long been just for professionals, but new technology has made a breeze for anyone. With glass medium and acrylic paints, you can create freehand designs such as the cactus—or paint the lizard with the pattern provided.

LIST of MATERIALS

* Glass beverage set, with glasses and pitcher
* Acrylic craft paints*: lt. green, dk. green, brown, terra-cotta
* Glass and tile medium*
* Artist's brush: No. 6 round, liner
* Miscellaneous items: tracing paper, pencil, paint palette, transparent tape

*(See Sources on pg. 159 for purchasing information.)

PITCHER

1 *Preparation:* Wash and dry glassware thoroughly. Remove any labels and label residue. See the Step 2 illustration to use pieces of tape to divide the pitcher into 6 equal segments for design placement.

2 *Lizard Pattern:* Trace lizard pattern to tracing paper. Refer to photo and illustration to tape pattern inside the pitcher neck. Use the No. 6 brush to paint the lizard design with the glass medium. Follow manufacturer's instructions; do not work medium too much. Let it dry first, then touch up, if necessary.

3 *Painting Lizard:* Follow paint manufacturer's instructions to paint the lizard over the glass medium with the No. 6 brush using the brown and terra-cotta paints. Refer to the photo to paint all the brown sections first, and then the terra-cotta; use No. 6 brush. Let paint dry, and add at least 1 more coat each of brown and terra-cotta.

4 *Cactus:* Paint a large cactus with the glass medium on the front of the pitcher. Refer to the photo, making the large center stalk first, and then side branches. Repeat to make 2 additional cacti on the pitcher sides.

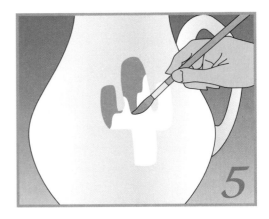

5 *Painting Cacti:* Paint cacti the same as the lizard in Step 3, mixing lt. and dk. green paints as desired. Let the paint dry, and use liner brush and brown paint to make spikes all over the cacti, as shown in the Glasses illustration below.

6 *Sealing:* Let the paint dry thoroughly, and seal the lizard and cacti with the glass medium. Follow manufacturer's instructions for number of coats and curing time. Also note manufacturer's recommendations and cautions for washing and use, because the paints are toxic and not food-safe.

7 *Other Methods:* There are 2 other methods of painting. The first is to create a frosted look by painting the designs with the glass medium only. The second is to mix the glass medium with the acrylic paints; follow manufacturer's instructions.

GLASSES

Follow Step 1 and Steps 4 and 6 of Pitcher to paint 3 cacti designs in every other segment around the glass. Follow Steps 2, 3 and 6 of Pitcher to paint the lizard on the glass base.

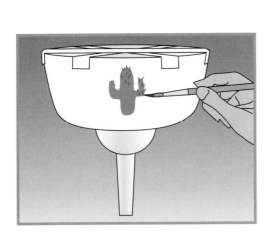

GLASS BASE
LIZARD
PATTERN

*R*ake in compliments by stitching autumn leaves and acorns on 7-mesh plastic canvas. Falling leaves and acorns stitched in golden autumn hues bring the season's richness into your home. The love you work into this project will warm the hearts of your family and friends for years to come.

LIST of MATERIALS

* ❊ 7-mesh plastic canvas, six sheets
* ❊ No. 16 tapestry needle
* ❊ Worsted weight yarn: rust, light brown, dark brown, dark avocado green, barn red, gold, off-white
* ❊ 1/16" (1.5 mm) wood dowel, 8" (20.5 cm)
* ❊ Brick
* ❊ Pattern Sheet
* ❊ Miscellaneous items: scissors, pencil, hot glue gun, craft knife

1 **General:** Refer to page 158 for Plastic Canvas Instructions and Stitches and Pattern Sheet for additional charts. Follow the bold outlines to cut the leaves and acorns from plastic canvas pieces. Refer to the photo to hot-glue stitched leaves and acorns to the coaster holder, planter, doorknob sign and doorstop cover.

2 **Oak Leaves:** Cut three 20x29-bar pieces of canvas. Work background of 2 leaves with barn red and 1 with gold using continental stitches. Overcast edges in dark brown.

3 **Maple Leaves:** Cut four 25x26-bar pieces of canvas. Work background of 2 leaves with gold, 1 with rust, and 1 with barn red using continental stitches. Overcast edges in dark brown.

MAPLE LEAF

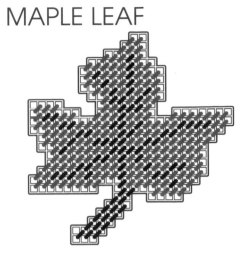

4 *Acorns:* Cut five 10x10-bar pieces of canvas. Work each acorn top with light brown slanted Gobelin stitches and the bottom with rust continental stitches. Overcast acorn with matching yarn.

5 *Coasters:* Cut four 25x25-bar pieces for coasters. Work background of coasters in off-white continental stitches; follow chart to stitch the rest. Overcast the edges with avocado green.

6 *Holder:* Cut two 11x13-bar pieces for sides, two 27x 13-bar pieces for front and back, and one 27x11-bar piece for bottom of coaster holder. Work the holder background in off-white Scotch stitches; follow charts to stitch the rest. Use avocado green to overcast the front, back and sides to bottom, then sides and top.

7 *Planter & Plant Poke:* Cut five 34x34-bar pieces of canvas for planter and repeat Step 6 Holder stitching instructions. For plant poke, glue rust maple leaf to 1 end of dowel.

8 *Doorknob Sign:* Cut one 33x71-bar piece of plastic canvas. Repeat Step 5 Coasters stitching instructions.

9 *Doorstop Cover:* Cut two 17x27-bar pieces for sides, two 57x27-bar pieces for front and back, and two 57x17-bar pieces for top and bottom. Work background in off-white Scotch stitches. Use avocado green to overcast the front, back and sides to the bottom. Place brick inside, then overcast the sides and top closed.

OAK LEAF

ACORN

This fresh plaid coordinates beautifully with the woodburned quilt rack colors, but it could be done in a solid, floral or print of your choice. Grosgrain ribbon for tie tabs makes hanging a snap—if you like velvet, satin or wire-edge better, substitute them instead.

Desired space between bottom of hanger & curtain top

Desired curtain width

Desired curtain length

1

1 Curtain Length: See the Step 1 illustration to measure from the curtain rod bottom to desired curtain length. Subtract the space desired (if any) between the rod lower edge and the curtain upper edge. Add 3½" (9 cm) for hem and ½" (1.3 cm) for seam allowance.

* Lightweight to mediumweight decorator fabric; to determine yardage see Steps 1 and 2 below
* 1¹¹/₁₆" (1.8 cm) wide ribbon for tie tabs; to determine yardage see Step 4 below

* Self-adhesive hook and loop tape
* Quilt rack or curtain rod

* Miscellaneous items: scissors or rotary cutter and cutting surface, iron, measuring tape, pencil, masking tape, straight pins, sewing machine and matching threads

2 *Curtain Width:* See the Step 1 illustration to measure the rod width, and multiply by 2, or more for even greater fullness. Measure the return, which is the distance the rod sticks out from the wall, and multiply by 2. To those 2 measurements, add 6" (15 cm) for hems. If you need to piece the fabric, add 1" (2.5 cm) for each seam, and stitch the pieces together in ½" (1.3 cm) seams.

3 *Cutting:* Cut fabric according to the measurements above. Cut a facing from same fabric, that is the curtain width by 2" (5 cm). At long lower edge, press up 1½" (3.8 cm) to the wrong side 2 times; use a straight stitch or blindstitch for a double-fold hem.

4 *Tie-Tab Yardage:* Pin ribbon strips over rod; mark desired length with pins. Tie a bow in ribbon ends; mark end of ribbon with pins. Measure total ribbon length; multiply by 2 for each tab. Space tie tabs 4" to 8" (10 to 20.5 cm) apart along curtain. Locate tabs along a repeating color bar or motif, such as shown in the photo. Multiply tab length by the number of tabs for total ribbon yardage.

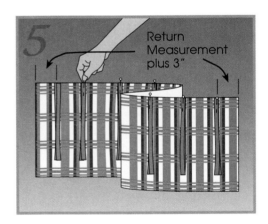

Return Measurement plus 3"

5 *Tie-Tab Placement:* Take Step 2 return measurement, and add 3" (7.5 cm). Measure this distance in from both sides of the curtain fabric. Pin-mark. See Step 5 illustration to pin 2 ribbons on top of each other with raw edges at top, and ribbons hanging down. Space remaining tabs evenly as planned in Step 4. Stitch tabs to fabric ³/₈" (1 cm) in from fabric and ribbon edges.

6 *Facing:* Press under ½" (1.3 cm) on 1 long edge of facing. Pin facing to curtain, right sides together, matching upper and side edges. Tie tabs will be sandwiched in between, with ribbons hanging down. Stitch ½" (1.3 cm) seam; trim facing seam allowance to ¼" (6 mm). Press facing to wrong side. Stitch facing to curtain from front side close to ½" (1.3 cm) folded edge. Press up 1½" (3.8 cm) twice on sides; stitch to make double-fold hems.

7 *Finishing:* Stitch across each set of tie tabs at desired ribbon length measurement from Step 4. Tie bows; trim ribbon tails. Hang curtain from rod. Secure ends to inside of quilt rack or rod bracket using self-adhesive hook and loop tape. Space tabs evenly on rod as desired; train curtain to fall in soft folds.

Techniques

Crochet

Abbreviations

beg . . . .Beginning
bet . . . .Between
bpdc . .Back Post Double Crochet
ch . . . . .Chain
dc . . . .Double Crochet
fpdc . . .Front Post Double Crochet
lp(s) . . .Loop(s)
rem . . . .Remaining
rep . . . .Repeat
rnd(s) . .Round(s)
sc . . . . .Single Crochet
sk . . . . .Skip
sl st . . . .Slip Stitch
sp(s) . . .Space(s)
st(s) . . . .Stitch(es)
tog . . . .Together
yo . . . . .Yarn Over
* . . . . . .Repeat following
        instructions a
        given number of
        times

Back Post Double Crochet (bpdc)

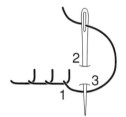

Yarn over, insert hook from back to front to back around post of next stitch, pull up loop. (Yarn over, pull through 2 loops on hook) twice.

Beginning Slip Knot

Begin with a slip knot on hook about 6" (15 cm) from end of yarn. Insert hook through loop; pull to tighten.

Chain Stitch (ch)

Yarn over, draw yarn through loop on hook to form new loop.

Double Crochet (dc)

1. For first row, yarn over, insert hook into 4th chain from hook. Yarn over; draw through 2 loops on hook.
2. Yarn over and pull yarn through last 2 loops on hook.

Front Post Double Crochet (fpdc)

Yarn over, insert hook from front to back to front around post of next stitch, draw up loop. (Yarn over, pull through 2 loops on hook) twice.

Forming Ring with a Slip Stitch

1. Insert hook in first chain.
2. Yarn over, and pull through all loops on hook.

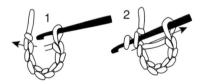

Single Crochet (sc)

1. For first row, insert hook into second chain from hook and draw up a loop.
2. Yarn over and draw through both loops on hook.

Slip Stitch (sl st)

Insert hook in stitch and draw up a loop. Yarn over and draw through both loops on hook.

Yarn Over (yo)

Wrap yarn over hook from back to front and proceed with specific stitch instructions.

General Instructions

1. Overcast the edges to prevent raveling. Fold the fabric in half vertically and horizontally to find the center, and mark it with a temporary stitch. If desired, place the fabric in an embroidery hoop. Find the center of the design by following arrows on the Chart. Count up and over to the top left stitch or specified point and begin stitching.

2. Each square on a Cross-Stitch Chart represents one square of even-weave fabric, unless otherwise indicated. Symbols correspond to the colors given in the Color Key.

3. Cut floss into 18" (46 cm) lengths. Separate the strands and use the number specified in the project. Stitching tends to twist the floss; allow

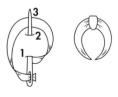

Blanket Stitch

Up at 1, down at 2, up at 3 with thread below needle; pull through.

Lazy Daisy Leaf Stitch

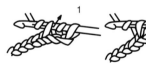

Up at 1, holding ribbon flat with thumb. Make loop, down near 1. Up at 2, make small anchor stitch over ribbon at 3.

Cross-Stitch

the needle to hang free from your work to untwist it from time to time.

4. To begin, do not knot the floss, but hold a tail on the back of the work until anchored by the first few stitches. To carry the floss across the back to another area to be stitched, weave the floss under previously worked stitches to new area, but do not carry the floss more than three or four stitches. To end the floss, run it under several stitches on the back, then cut it. Do not use knots.

5. Work all cross-stitches first, then any additional stitches, including backstitches. Work in horizontal rows wherever possible. To make vertical stitches, complete each cross stitch before moving to the next one.

6. When stitching is completed, wash the fabric in warm sudsy water if needed. Roll it in a terrycloth towel to remove excess moisture. Press it facedown on another terrycloth towel to dry.

Stitches

Backstitch
Up at 1, down at 2, up at 3, down at 4, stitching back to meet prior stitch.

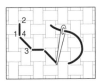

Cross-Stitch
Work first half of each stitch left to right; complete each stitch right to left.

Cross Stitch Linen
Begin over a vertical thread, stitching from lower left to upper right corner over 2 threads; complete stitch right to left.

Smyrna Cross Linen
Up at odd, down at even numbers, working in numerical sequence over 6 threads.

Embroidery

Blanket Stitch Corner 1
Make a diagonal blanket stitch. Tack stitch at corner, insert needle through loop; pull taut.

Blanket Stitch Corner 2
To work corner, use same center hole to work stitches 1, 2, and 3.

Running Stitch
Up at odd, down at even numbers for specified length.

Straight Diagonal Stitch
Up at 1, down at 2.

Ribbon Embroidery

Needle Lock
To lock ribbon on needle, insert threaded needle ½" from end of ribbon. Pull on opposite end to lock.

French Knot
Up at 1, wrap ribbon around needle specified number of times, down near 1.

Spider Web Rose Stitch

With floss, stitch 5 spokes for the anchor. With ribbon, come up in center and work in an over and under pattern around spokes, keeping ribbon loose and letting it twist. Fill in to cover spokes.

Looped Petal Stitch
Up at 1, form loop, holding loop flat with left thumb. Pull ends on top of each other. Down at 2, pulling ribbon to make first petal loop. Repeat to make desired number of petals.

Stem Stitch
Up at 1, down at 2, up at 3, keeping thread to left of needle and working slightly slanted stitches along the line of design.

General Instructions

1. Sanding: Many projects are done on wood, and so must be sanded. If painting on a non-wood surface, make sure it is clean and dry. Begin the process with coarse-grit sandpaper, and end with finer grits. A 150-grit sandpaper will put finish smoothness on surfaces, such as preparing for staining or sanding. A 220-grit extra-fine sandpaper is good for smoothing stained or painted wood before varnishing, or between coats. Use a tack cloth—a treated, sticky cheesecloth—to lightly remove sanding dust after each step. Don't rub over the surface or you will leave a sticky residue on the wood. Wood files, sanding blocks and emery boards can be used to sand hard-to-reach places and curves.

2. Transferring: Place pattern on surface or wood, following direction for grainline. For pattern outlines, such as for cutting your own pieces, use a pencil to trace around pattern piece onto wood. Trace lightly, so wood is not indented. To transfer detail lines, you can use pencil, chalk, transfer paper or graphite paper. Ink beads over many waxed transfer papers, so if you plan to use fine-line permanent-ink markers for detail lines, be sure to use graphite or wax-free transfer paper. Transfer as few lines as possible, painting freehand instead. Do not press hard, or surface may be indented. Use eraser to remove pencil lines, damp cloth on chalk, and paint thinner or soap and water on graphite.

To use pencil or chalk, rub the wrong side of traced pattern. Shake off any loose lead; lay pattern penciled or chalk-side down on wood, and retrace pattern with a pencil or stylus.

To use transfer or graphite paper, place paper facedown on wood, then place pattern on top. Lightly trace over pattern lines. Lay a piece of wax paper on top of pattern to be traced. This protects your original traced pattern and also lets you see what you have traced.

3. Brushes: The size should always correspond in size to the area being painted, preferably with the largest brush that will fit the design area. The brush should also reflect the technique being done, which is usually suggested in craft project directions.

4. Extender: Acrylic extender is a medium to add to acrylic paints to increase their open time. Open time refers to the amount of time in which you can mix and blend the paints before they begin to dry. Those familiar with oil paints are most concerned with this, or if you are doing very complex designs with a great deal of shading.

Techniques

Adding a Wash:
Dilute the paint with five parts water to one part paint (or whatever proportion is requested) and mix well. Load the brush, and blot excess paint on brush onto a paper towel. Fill in the area to be painted, giving transparent coverage. A wash can also be used for shading or highlighting large areas.

Basecoating:
Applying the first coat of paint to a prepared surface, usually covering the surface and all edges in entirety. Sometimes two coats of paint are recommended. Basecoating is usually done with a flat or sponge brush.

Comma Strokes

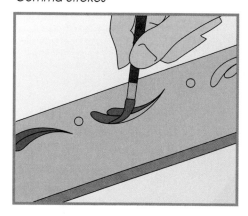

Dots

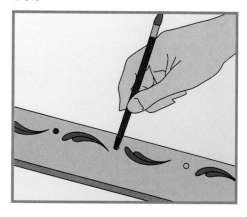

Double Loading:
This is the same as side loading, except two colors are loaded, one on each side of the brush. The colors gradually blend into one another in the middle of the brush.

Comma Strokes:
This is a stroke that is in the shape of a comma, with a large head and long, curvy thin tail. They come in all shapes and sizes. Begin painting up at the round head and curve down to the tail. Comma strokes require practice before they look right.

Dots:
Dots can be made by dipping the end of the paintbrush or stylus or even a toothpick in paint and then touching it gently on the painted surface. This technique can create perfect eyes or dots better than any brush tip.

Dry-Brushing:
This technique is used to achieve a soft or aged look; many times it is used to blush cheeks. Dip dry brush tips in a small amount of paint (undiluted for heavy coverage and diluted for transparent coverage). Wipe on paper towel until almost no paint is left. Then gently brush on the surface.

Highlighting:
Highlighting is the reverse of shading, causing an area to be more prominent. Thus a lighter color, such as white, is often loaded on a flat brush and used for highlighting. Highlighting is also sometimes done with a liner brush, by painting a straight line with a light color over an area to give a dimensional appearance.

Shading:
Shading is done with a color darker than the main color, making an area recede into the background. It is frequently used on edges of designs and done with the side load or floating technique. On an orange background, the brush is loaded with rust, and pulled along the edge, with the paint edge of brush where color is to be darkest.

Side Loading or Floating Color:
Side loading or floating is usually done with a flat or shader brush. Dip or load brush in water; then lightly blot on paper towel to release some moisture. Load or pull one side of the brush through paint. Blend paint on a mixing surface so the color begins to move across the bristles, and is dark on one edge, but light on the other. Make sure to get the paint well blended before actually painting on the surface. Another method is to thin the paint (see below) and mix it well. Load the paint by dipping one corner in, and blending well on a mixing surface, as above.

Stippling:
This is a stenciling technique, and is very similar to dry-brushing, except it gives a more fuzzy or textured look. Stencil, fabric or stippler brushes may be used, or any old scruffy brush. Dip just brush tips in a small amount of paint, then blot on paper towel until brush is almost dry. Apply the paint to the surface by pouncing up and down with the bristle tips until desired coverage is achieved.

Thinning:
Add drops of water and mix until the paint is of an inklike consistency. Sometimes a specific mix of water and paint is requested.

Highlighting

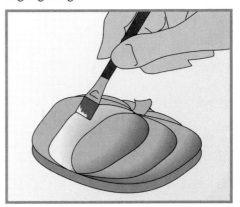

Shading

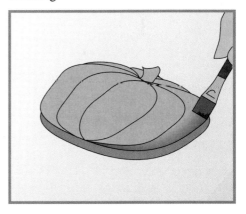

Side Loading or Floating Color

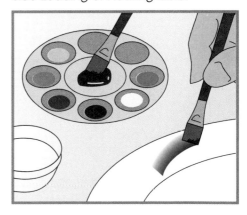

General Instructions

1. Each line on a Plastic Canvas Chart represents one bar of plastic canvas.

2. To cut plastic canvas, count the lines on the graph and cut the canvas accordingly, cutting up to, but not into, the bordering bars. Follow the bold outlines where given. Use a craft knife to cut small areas.

3. To stitch, do not knot the yarn, but hold a tail in back and anchor with the first few stitches. To end yarn, weave tail under stitches on back, then cut it. Do not stitch over edge bars.

4. When finished stitching individual pieces, finish edges and join pieces as specified with an overcast stitch.

Stitches

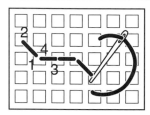

Backstitch
Up at 1, down at 2, up at 3, down at 4, stitching back to meet prior stitch.

Beaded Half Cross Stitch
Stitch from lower left, slip on bead, stitch down at upper right over 1 bar of canvas.

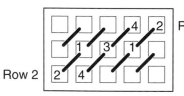

Continental Stitch
Work Row 1, up at 1, down at 2, up at 3, down at 4, working toward left. Work Row 2, up at 1, down at 2, working toward right in established sequence.

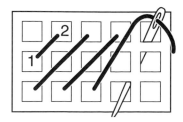

Gobelin Stitch
Up at 1, down at 2, working diagonal stitches over two or more bars in direction indicated on graph.

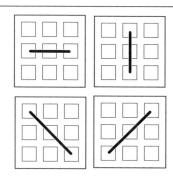

Long/Diagonal Stitch
Stitch over specified number of bars as indicated on graph.

Overcast Stitch
Use a whipping motion over the outer bars to cover or join canvas edges.

Scotch Stitch
Up at odd, down at even numbers, making a square design with the longest diagonal stitch across center of the square and graduated lengths on each side.

Hanging Sleeve:
1. Cut a piece from backing fabric or muslin 2" shorter than quilt width by 10" (25.5 cm). Stitch double-fold 1/2" (1.3 cm) hems on both short ends.

2. Stitch the long ends in a 1/2" (1.3 cm) seam, right sides together; press seam open. Turn right side out; press sleeve flat with seam centered.

3. Pin sleeve on quilt back at upper edge. Hand-stitch all around, going through backing and batting layers only.

Yo Yos

1. Cut circles from assorted fabrics in sizes as directed. Sew running stitches by hand or long machine stitches for gathering 1/4" (6 mm) from edge all around.

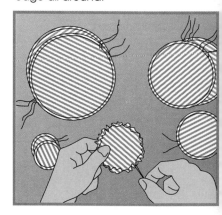

2. Do not knot; leave long thread tail(s). See illustration to evenly pull thread(s) tight to gather at center, turning circle right side out.

3. Flatten and shape yo yo; knot thread and tuck tails into center.

Sources

Most of these items are available at your local craft retail stores. If you are having difficulties locating items, or live far from a retail store, please reference the sources listed below.

Page 6   *Modern Mini Clocks:* Decoupaged: Mini Mantel Clock #53505 and Mini Arabic Bezel Movement #908. Faux Marquetry: Mini Desk Clock #53506 and Mini Roman Bezel Movement #907. Gold Foiled: Mini Wide Arch Clock #53504 and Mini Roman Bezel Movement #907. Clocks courtesy of Walnut Hollow. Call 800-950-5101 or write 1409 State Road 23, Dodgeville, WI 53533-2112.

Page 11   *Doilies Sweatshirt:* Wimpole Street Creations doilies from Barrett House, PO Box 540585, N. Salt Lake, UT 84054-0585, 801-299-0700.

Page 18   *Stamped Apple Accessories:* Contact Kunin Felt, a Foss Mfg. Co., for Kreative Kanvas™ floorcloth, placemat and coasters at 603-929-6100 or write to PO 5000, Hampton, NH 03843. Gesso, paints and varnish by Liquitex. Designed by Betsy Edwards.

Page 22   *Beaded Bracelet Watch:* Beads from The Beadery® Craft Products, PO Box 178, Hope Valley, RI 02832, 401-539-2432.

Page 26   *Screen Door & Picket Fence:* Screen Door #11227, Moon Appliqué #16903, Little Wood Birdhouses 3 pkgs. # 30012. Slim Picket Fence #11209, Little Wood Small Leaves 6 pkgs. #30041. Products courtesy of Walnut Hollow. Call 800-950-5101 or write 1409 State Road 23, Dodgeville, WI 53533-2112. Designed by Michelle Schmitz and Allison Stilwell respectively.

Page 36   *Sunflower Bird Bath:* #2501 Sunflowers and #2515 Blue Bow Border rub-on Transfers from the Indoor/Outdoor Accents™ line by Loew-Cornell, 201-836-7070, 563 Chestnut Ave., Teaneck, NJ 07666-2490, loewcornel@aol.com. DecoArt™ Patio Paints in Daisy Cream, Sunflower Yellow and Clear Coat for sealer were used. Project courtesy of Loew-Cornell.

Page 46   *Indoor & Outdoor Planter Boxes:* Prestained Square Planter Boxes: 6" (15 cm) Weathered Gray #64530 and 9" (23 cm) Shale Green #63531. Rubber Stampede leaf, fern and sun stamps. Fish and flower planters: #3585, tissue box #11360P. Boxes courtesy of Walnut Hollow. Call 800-950-5101 or write 1409 State Road 23, Dodgeville, WI 53533-2112. Designed by Allison Stilwell.

Page 50   *Elegance for the Bath:* Daniel Enterprises Crafter's Pride Aida ovals (14-count 4" x 5" (10 x 12.5 cm) and 18-count 2³/₄" x 3¹/₂" (7 x 9 cm)) available from the Stitch and Frame Shop, 1627 Celanese, Rock Hill, SC 29732, 800-636-6341.

Page 52   *Faux-Stone Candleholders & Beaded Bobèches:* Krylon® Make It Stone! finish in charcoal sand with Clear Coat Protector was used on the candleholders. Brass candle inserts and glass or acrylic ring cups are available in candle shops and some craft stores.

Page 54   *Yo Yo Placemats & Napkin Rings:* Wimpole Street Creations premade yo yos from Barrett House, PO Box 540585, N. Salt Lake, UT 84054-0585, 801-299-0700.

Page 55   *Honeycomb Napkin Rings* MPR Associates, Inc. honeycomb paper sheets from Cottage Crafts at 800-454-3331.

Page 62   *Sunflower Suite Storage:* Call 800-554-4661 for Highsmith® Corruboard® BASICS storage products: magazine file #25873K, craft cubby #24093K and drawers #24094K, and supply mate #24123K. Products courtesy of Highsmith, Inc.

Page 74   *Document Box & Memory Album Covers:* Document Box #3212, rubber stamp designs by Personal Stamp Exchange. Leaf Album: 6" x 9" (15 x 23 cm) Nostalgic Memory Album Cover #3705, leaf rubber stamp design by Personal Stamp Exchange. 10" x 12" (25.5 x 30.5 cm) Contemporary Memory Album Cover #3700, Classic Dimensions long scroll #16406, round #16502, and 2 squares, #16113. Contemporary Cover designed by Connie Sheerin. Call Personal Stamp Exchange at 707-588-8058 for nearest stamp supplier. Document box and album covers courtesy of Walnut Hollow. Call 800-950-5101 or write 1409 State Road 23, Dodgeville, WI 53533-2112.

Page 76   *Pine Needle Basket:* For ordering information about pine needles contact Kathleen Peelen Krebs at Pine Design 510-527-5692.

Page 84   *Mosaic Bottle & Picture Frame:* 1" (2.5 cm) mosaic tiles in various color families, grout, adhesive, nippers and other accessories are by Mosaic Mercantile, PO Box 1550, Livingston, MT 59047, 406-222-0990, www.mosaicmerc.com.

Page 96   *Rubber Stamp Notecards:* Stamp Affair rubber stamps, watercolor brush markers and Pad Magic™ olive green (SP-616) ink pad are available at 1-800 4INKPAD. Stamp design numbers: Girl with braids (J1086), flower button (M1097), heart button (M1105), star button (M1104), small sunflower (M1106), large sunflower (J787), apple (M343), pear (M858).

Page 100   *Victorian Barrettes:* Oval pillow clips are still stocked, though not listed in their catalog, by Barrett House, PO Box 540585, N. Salt Lake, UT 84054-0585, 801-299-0700.

CONTINUED

Sources CONTINUED

Page 108 _Mom's Recipe Book & Tea Jar:_ Friendly Clay™ Millefiori Quilt Squares with Checkerboard/Daisy design, and Cotton Press® cotton linter sheets, additive and Terra-Cotta Mini Mold with Tea Time design by American Art Clay Co. Inc. For catalog call 800-374-1600. Recipe book and tea jar courtesy of American Art Clay Co. Inc.

Page 118 _Classic Window:_ Plaid's Gallery Glass products were used to create the window designed by Laura Brunson. Contact Plaid at 800-842-4197 for: Gallery Glass™ styrene blanks #16052, liquid leading #16082, window colors: crystal clear #16081, amber #16020 and clear frost #16022.

Page 120 _Dish Towel Pillow:_ Wimpole Street Creations dish towels, yo yos and doilies from Barrett House, PO Box 540585, N. Salt Lake, UT 84054-0585, 801-299-0700.

Page 128 _Paisley Penny Vest:_ Call National Nonwovens at 800-333-3469 ext. 214 for retailers who carry WoolFelt® pre-sewn vest and felt by the yard or 9" x 12" (23 x 30.5 cm) squares. Norwegian blue 579, chartreuse green 715, bright red 938, dark orange 821, and gold 416. Designed by National Nonwovens.

Page 130 _Country Birdhouse Lamp:_ Medium Flock Home Birdhouse #11102 and Little Wood Small Leaves #30041. Products courtesy of Walnut Hollow. Call 800-950-5101 or write 1409 State Road 23, Dodgeville, WI 53533-2112.

Page 132 _Easy Triangle Sampler Quilt:_ Half Square Triangle Paper™ by Quiltime and hand-dyed pink triangle fabric from Colorful Quilts and Textiles, 2817 North Hamline Avenue, Roseville, MN 55113-1715, 612-628-9664. Designed by Susan Stein.

Page 138 _Basket Bouquet Quilt Rack:_ Quilt Rack from Cabin Comforts, 8403 W. Farm Road 84, Willard, MO 65871, 417-887-9465. Creative woodburner #5567, Cone Point Tip #5596, and oil pencils from Walnut Hollow, 1409 State Road 23, Dodgeville, WI 53533, 800-950-5101. Designed by Vicki Schreiner.

Page 142 _Grapes Table Runner & Napkin Rings:_ Plaid Grape Vine Decorator Blocks™ and Decorator Glazes™ were used on the table runner, 800-842-4197. Contact Creative Beginnings for brass charms and rings at 800-367-1739.

Page 148 _Painted Glass Beverage Set:_ Plaid Folk Art® Glass & Tile Painting Medium and Acrylic colors were used, 800-842-4197.

Credits

Crafts in a FLASH!

Created by: The Editors of Cowles Creative Publishing, Inc. in cooperation with _Crafts Magazine_ – PJS Publications Incorporated.

COWLES
Creative Publishing

President: Iain Macfarlane
Group Director, Book Development: Zoe Graul
Creative Director: Lisa Rosenthal
Senior Managing Editor: Elaine Perry

Project Manager: Tracy Stanley
Art Director: Mark Jacobson
Project Editor: Deborah Howe
Copy Editor: Janice Cauley
Illustrator: Earl R. Slack
Desktop Publishing Specialist: Laurie Kristensen
Print Production Manager: Kim Gerber

America's #1
Crafts
Magazine

Editor: Miriam Olson

IBSN 0-86573-195-0

Printed on American paper by:
 World Color Press
01 00 99 98 / 5 4 3 2 1

Cowles Creative Publishing, Inc. offers a variety of how-to books. For information write:
 Cowles Creative Publishing
 Subscriber Books
 5900 Green Oak Drive
 Minnetonka, MN 55343